Hey Mom...I'll Cook Dinner!

Recipes that Turn a Kid Into the Family Chef

by Anita K. Nobles

Cover Design and Graphics on pages 11, 15, 18, 20, 42, 53, 74 & 94 by Bebe Betz Pinkley
Page Design and Graphics by Art Terry,

To My Dad

Stan Jones

Thanks for setting the standards by which we live and for being the best business partner a daughter could ever have.

Impressions Ink
5147 Patrick Henry Dr.
Memphis, TN 38134

ISBN 1-882626-21-4
United States

Impressions Ink books are available at your local bookstores or giftshops. For information on the retailers in your area or to place an order please contact Impressions Ink, 5147 Patrick Henry Dr., Memphis, Tennessee, 38134 or call (901)388-5382 or (800)388-5382

Printed in the United States of America

Introduction

"Hi. Did you get home from school okay?" "Yeah Mom, I'm home-safe and sound. Want me to start dinner?"

Then would come the over-the-phone-from-miles-away directions of how to prepare dinner. I often wondered when we hung up if she wondered just what she would find when she came home. I was 11 years old when I began "starting" dinner and I didn't know what a loaf pan looked like, let alone a colander.

"Hey Mom...I'll Cook Dinner!" is a collection of healthy recipes that kids will enjoy eating as well as preparing. We had our focus group of kids, 10 years old and up, tell us what they liked to cook and what they liked to eat. They went on to tell us that they didn't want to spend more than an hour in the kitchen preparing dinner. They confessed to those things they most often forget to do in the kitchen (like turn-off the oven). We used all of this information as the foundation for this book. Our team consulted with Susan A. Helms, Coordinator of the Mid-South **SAFE KIDS** Coalition to find out where and how most injuries occur in the kitchen. The Coalition provided a Safety Check List for parents to review with children. We have included it on page 4. All the recipes have been written so that no stovetop cooking (except simmering soups) is involved. This book is jam packed with helpful information and facts. In the back we added:

> **an oven magnet (for reminding)**
> **a tape measure (for measuring)**
> **a detailed shopping list (for simplifying)**
> **an Important Telephone Numbers List (for the fridge.)**

Only parents can determine when their children are ready for cooking alone. When they are ready, "Hey Mom...I'll Cook Dinner!" is an another excellent tool from Impressions Ink, for helping your child grow up.

Note: *Our microwave recipes are parameters for cooking and cooking times may differ for your own microwave.*

Safety Check List

Follow these simple measures to lower the risk of serious injury.

1. Set up a schedule for checking and changing the batteries in smoke detectors.

2. Plan and practice fire escape routes every six months.

3. Check hot water temperature, be sure it is no higher than 120° to avoid scalds.

4. Post Important Telephone Numbers List near the phone or on the fridge.

5. Build a First Aid Kit and make sure everyone knows where it is kept. (Recipe on page 124)

6. Replace supplies when used.

7. Take a first aid and CPR course so that you are prepared if an emergency happens.

Mid-South SAFE KIDS Coalition is a group of businesses, civic groups and individuals dedicated to the prevention of unintentional childhood injuries. It is headquarted at Le Bonheur Children's Medical Center in Memphis, Tennessee.

IMPORTANT TELEPHONE NUMBERS

POLICE, FIRE, AMBULANCE _____**911**_____

Mother's Work Number _____   Father's Work Number _____

Neighbor _____   Phone Number _____

Friend _____   Phone Number _____

Relative _____   Phone Number _____

Other _____   Phone Number _____

Doctor _____   Phone Number _____

Poison Control Center/Emergency _____

Your Telephone Number _____

Your Address _____

Simple Directions to Your House _____

Kitchen Tips to Review with Children.

◆ Wash hands before handling and mixing food.

◆ Wear a T-shirt to keep clothes clean.

◆ Assemble ingredients on one side of working area and utensils on the other before starting.

◆ Clean up as you go to prevent a huge cleanup. Use one bowl, wash and rewash, etc.

◆ Keep hot foods and drinks away from edge of counters and tables.

◆ Use a pot holder or oven mitt for handling hot containers.

◆ Appliances should be kept away from water. Unplug appliances not in use.

◆ Measure dry ingredients over wax paper for easy clean up.

◆ Measure wet ingredients over sink for easy clean up.

◆ To use a grater, hold object by the fingertips to avoid grating knuckles.

◆ Use a wooden spoon to stir so that heat is not transmitted through the handle.

◆ Use a blender as directed.

◆ Use caution when removing food from Microwave or Oven. Microwave ovens should be set at countertop or table level.

◆ Use a mixer on Medium speed and a deep bowl for mixing ingredients.

◆ Use a cutting board for chopping and slicing.

◆ Use kitchen shears for cutting when possible.

◆ Use a sharpened knife when necessary and always point the blade down and away from the body.

How To Do It!
• Drain Foods
• Cook Bacon
• Cook Chicken
• Melt Butter
• Soften Butter
  or Cream Cheese
• Coat with Crumbs
• Pound Meat
• Drizzle
• Grease Pan

See Page 127

Table of Contents

Vegetables and Side Dishes

Main Dishes

Breakfast and Brunch Dishes

Desserts and Cookie Bars

Finger Pizzas

1 pound ground sausage
1 pound process American cheese, grated
2 tablespoons ketchup
1 teaspoon Worcestershire sauce
1/2 teaspoon dried whole oregano
1/4 teaspoon caraway seeds
1/8 teaspoon garlic powder
2 (8-ounce) loaves party rye bread

20 Min.

Preparation Time!

Place ground sausage in a Microwave safe dish, cover and Microwave on HIGH, stirring every 2 minutes, until done. Be sure to cook thoroughly. Add cheese, ketchup, Worcestershire sauce, oregano, caraway seeds, and garlic powder. Mix and Microwave until cheese is melted. Spread a teaspoon of mixture on each slice of rye bread; bake on an ungreased baking sheet at 350° for 7 minutes. Serve warm.

Fun Food Fact: *94% of all home gardeners plant tomatoes. It is the most popular vegetable among gardeners.*

Quick Ham Sandwiches

1 1/2 cups finely chopped cooked ham
1 (4-ounce) jar chopped pimento, drained
1/2 cup chopped parsley
1/2 cup mayonnaise

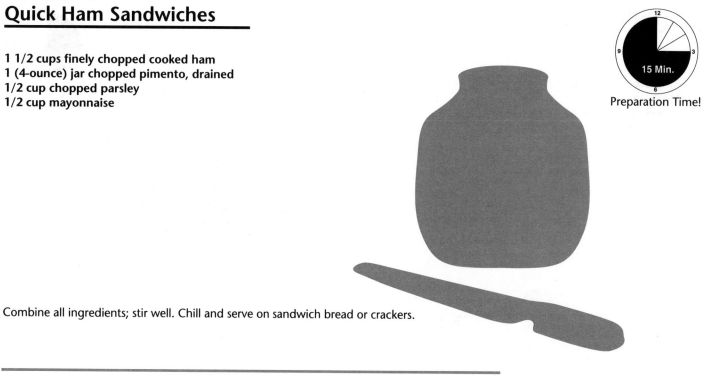

15 Min.

Preparation Time!

Combine all ingredients; stir well. Chill and serve on sandwich bread or crackers.

Fun Food Fact: *A bagel is a round yeast bun with a hole in the middle. It is boiled first and then baked.*

Full Moon Rolls

1 (8-ounce) can crescent dinner rolls
1 (8-ounce) package cream cheese, softened
1/2 cup finely chopped ham
2 tablespoons green olives, chopped
1 tablespoon green onion, chopped
Paprika

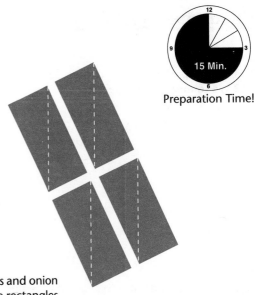

15 Min.

Preparation Time!

Separate dough into four rectangles. Press the perforation to close. Mix the ham, olives and onion with the cream cheese. Spread the rectangles with the cream cheese mixture. Roll the rectangles up starting with the small end and seal the edges. Cut each roll into four slices. Sprinkle with paprika. Place on ungreased cookie sheet and bake at 350° for 20 minutes or until golden brown.

Fun Food Fact: *Americans love cheese. The total amount of cheese consumed in America averages 26 pounds per person per year.*

Cucumber Boats

2 medium cucumbers
1 (3-ounce) package cream cheese, softened
1 (2 1/4 -ounce) can deviled ham

Peel cucumbers and cut in half lengthwise and scoop out seeds. Combine cream cheese and deviled ham. Mix well and spoon into cucumber halves. Cover with plastic and refrigerate for 2 hours. Cut cucumber halves into half and then slice the quarters lengthwise. Yields 16 pieces.

Fun Food Fact: Today salsa outsells ketchup as the number one condiment in America.

Fresh Veggies and Dip

1 (8-ounce) package Neufchatel cheese, softened
1/2 cup mayonnaise
3 tablespoons milk
3 green onions, chopped
1 tablespoon parsley flakes
3/4 teaspoon dill
1/4 teaspoon garlic salt

2 cups cauliflower florets
2 cups broccoli florets
4 stalks celery
3 large carrots
2 small zucchini
2 small yellow crookneck squash

20 Min.

Preparation Time!

Mix cheese, mayonnaise, milk, onions, parsley, dill, and garlic salt. Blend well. Chill. Wash cauliflower and broccoli, pat dry and set aside. Wash other vegetables and slice celery and carrots into sticks for dipping. Slice zucchini and yellow squash into 1/4 inch rounds. Arrange all vegetables on large tray with a bowl for dip in the middle.

Fun Food Fact: *The carrot is a long orange root that has many uses in recipes. It can be served raw, boiled, added to casseroles, made into puddings and soups, and added to cakes.*

15

Pizza Snackers

1 pound ground beef
1 (1.5 ounce) package dry spaghetti sauce mix
1/4 dried whole oregano
1 (6-ounce) can tomato paste
4 English muffins, split and toasted
32 slices pepperoni
1 cup shredded Mozzarella cheese

Preparation Time!

Crumble beef into a Microwave safe dish and cover with plastic. Microwave on HIGH, stirring every 2 minutes until done. Drain. Combine spaghetti sauce mix, oregano and tomato paste; add to beef. Stir well. Cover and Microwave on HIGH for 2 minutes or until hot. Place 4 muffin halves on a paper napkin lined plate. Spoon meat mixture over muffin halves and top with 4 pepperoni slices. Microwave on HIGH for 1 minute, turning the plate one half turn after 30 seconds. Sprinkle shredded cheese on top and Microwave on HIGH for 30 seconds. Repeat with other 4 muffin halves. Yields 8 servings.

Fun Food Fact: *The first restaurant selling pizza in America was Gennaro Lombardi's on Spring Street in New York City. The world's largest pizza was made in 1971 by Lorenzo Amato, owner of a restaurant in Tallahassee, Florida. It was 10,000 square feet of pizza.*

Chicken Squares

35 Min.

Preparation Time!

1 (3-ounce) package cream cheese, softened
2 tablespoons butter or margarine, softened
2 cups cooked chopped chicken, or 2 (5-ounce) cans boned chicken
1/4 teaspoon salt
1/8 teaspoon pepper
2 tablespoons milk
1 tablespoon chopped onion
1 tablespoon chopped pimento
1 tablespoon chopped parsley
1 (8-ounce) can crescent dinner rolls
1 egg, beaten
3/4 cup crushed seasoned croutons

In a bowl, blend cream cheese and butter. Add cooked chicken, salt, pepper, milk, onion, pimento and parsley. Blend well. Open refrigerated crescent rolls and separate dough into 4 rectangles. Press the preforations that run from one corner to another closed to seal, so that you have a rectangular piece of dough. Spoon about 4 heaping tablespoons of chicken mixture onto each piece of dough. Pull the corners up and twist them together and seal the edges. This makes a little square chicken bundle. Place bundles on an ungreased cookie sheet. Brush them with the beaten egg and sprinkle with crushed croutons. Bake at 350° for 25 minutes or until golden brown.

Fun Food Fact: *Sushi is a Japanese method of serving food. Most of the fish is served raw or only slightly cooked. It is served on a bar of rice or wrapped with seaweed. California rolls are popular among sushi eaters. They are made with avocado, crabmeat and cucumbers wrapped in rice. Sushi is eaten with the fingers...Japanese finger food!*

Pimento Cheese Spread

15 Min.

Preparation Time!

2 cups grated Cheddar cheese
1 cup grated American cheese
1/2 teaspoon finely chopped onion
1 (2-ounce) jar of diced pimentos, drained
1/3 cup mayonnaise

In a bowl mix cheese, onion, pimentos and mayonnaise. Blend well. Serve on crackers, in celery boats, or spread on sandwich bread. Refrigerate until ready to serve.

Fun Food Fact: *Americans consume over 8 1/2 pounds of salt per year on foods.*

Ranch Dinner Bread

1 loaf of french bread
2 teaspoons dry ranch salad dressing mix.
1/2 cup butter or margarine

Preparation Time!

15 Min.

Make deep cuts into the bread every 1 1/2". Cutting down to the bottom, but not through. Place dry seasoning and butter in Microwave safe dish. Cover and Microwave for 2 minutes or until butter is melted. Mix and brush onto both sides of bread slices. Wrap bread in foil and bake at 350° for 10 minutes or until bread is warm. Yields 6 servings. Note: Everybody wants seconds of this bread so make a little extra.

Fun Food Fact: The grocery cart we wheel around the store was introduced in 1937 by Sylvan Goldman of Oklahoma City, Oklahoma. Just one more time-saving device created by some imaginative individual.

Cheesy Biscuits

2 cups self-rising flour
1/3 cup butter or margarine, softened
1 cup buttermilk
1/2 teaspoon chopped parsley
1 1/2 cup grated Cheddar cheese

Preparation Time!

Cut butter into flour until mixture looks coarse like crumbs; add buttermilk, parsley and cheese. Mix well and drop spoonfuls, 2 inches apart, onto a greased cookie sheet. Bake at 425° for 15 minutes or until golden brown. Yields 18.

Fun Food Fact: *Cheddar came from the village of Cheddar in Somerset, England. Cheddar cheese has been made there since the 1500's.*

Golden Fruit Muffins

1 (8 1/4-ounce) can crushed pineapple-undrained
Milk
2 cups all-purpose flour
1/3 cup firmly packed brown sugar
1 tablespoon baking powder
1/2 teaspoon salt
1/4 cup sugar
1/2 teaspoon ground cinnamon
3/4 cup grated carrots
1/4 cup golden raisins
1/4 cup vegetable oil
1 egg, beaten
1/2 teaspoon vanilla extract

Preparation Time!

Drain pineapple, reserving juice. Add enough milk to pineapple juice to make 3/4 cup liquid. Combine all the ingredients in a large mixing bowl. Stir until moistened and spoon mixture into greased muffin pans, filling 2/3 of each cup. Bake at 375° for 25 minutes or until golden brown. Yields 12 muffins.

Fun Food Fact: *The Aztecs were some of the first people to eat avocados. The first avocados were brought to Florida in 1833. California is the leading producer of this fruit in America.*

Apple Annie Muffins

1 1/2 cups peeled, chopped tart apples
2 cups all-purpose flour
1/2 cup sugar
1 tablespoon baking powder
1/2 teaspoon salt
1/2 teaspoon ground cinnamon
1/4 teaspoon ground nutmeg
1 cup milk
1/4 cup vegetable oil
1 egg beaten
1/4 cup sugar
1/2 teaspoon ground cinnamon

Preparation Time!

Place 1 cup of the apples in a mixing bowl. Add flour, sugar, baking powder, salt, cinnamon and nutmeg. Mix well. Combine milk, oil, and egg. Add to flour mixture, stirring just until moist. Spoon batter into greased muffin cups filling 2/3 full. Combine remaining apple, 1/4 cup sugar and 1/2 teaspoon cinnamon. Spoon mixture over batter in muffin cups and bake at 350° for 25 minutes. Yield 12 muffins.

Fun Food Fact: *A funnel cake is a deep fried pastry made by dripping batter through a funnel into hot oil. This Pennsylvania Dutch breakfast dish was swirled in a spiral in hot fat and then served with sugar or maple syrup. Today you can find funnel cakes at fairs and open-air events.*

22

Cheesy Bread Slices

1 loaf french bread
1 stick butter or margarine, softened
1 cup Monterey Jack cheese
1 cup Cheddar cheese

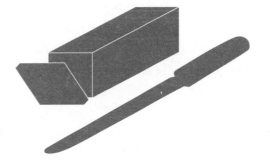

Slice french bread into 1 1/2" thick slices and arrange on cookie sheet. Spread each slice with butter and sprinkle with cheeses. Bake at 350° for 10 minutes or until cheese is melted and starting to get crispy on the edges. Yields 8 servings.

Fun Food Fact: *Americans drink most beverages with ice to cool them down. Europeans tend to consume more beverages at room temperature without ice.*

Garden Crisp Salad

4 cups torn Romaine lettuce
2 tomatoes, chopped
1 cucumber peeled and sliced
4 green onions chopped
1/4 cup grated carrot
croutons
1/3 cup grated cheese (Cheddar, American or Monterey Jack)

15 Min.

Preparation Time!

Combine lettuce, tomatoes, cucumber, onion and carrot. Toss gently. Add croutons and grated cheese. Serve with favorite salad dressings. Yields 4 servings

Fun Food Fact: *Fortune cookies are an American invention. David Jung of Los Angeles was the first baker to give them away with messages of hope stuffed inside.*

24

Greek Salad

1 head Romaine lettuce
1 cucumber
1/2 cup chopped green pepper
3/4 cup crumbled feta cheese

1/2 cup olive oil
3 tablespoons lemon juice
1/4 teaspoon salt
1/4 teaspoon pepper
Black olives

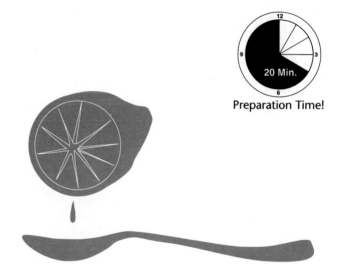

20 Min.

Preparation Time!

Wash lettuce leaves well and cut into pieces. Peel cucumber and cut into thin slices. Combine lettuce, cucumber, green pepper and cheese and toss gently. In a small bowl mix olive oil, lemon juice, salt and pepper. Serve on salad (as dressing) just before serving. Garnish salad with black olives.

Fun Food Fact: *During World War I people planted "Liberty Gardens" to supply their own vegetables and produce. This freed up more of the farm-produced vegetables and fruits to be sent to troops stationed overseas.*

Gazpacho Salad

4 large tomatoes
2 cucumbers
1 green pepper
1 purple onion

1/3 cup red wine vinegar
1/3 cup tomato sauce
1/2 cup olive oil
1 teaspoon lemon juice
Salt
Pepper
croutons

20 Min.

Preparation Time!

Peel and chop tomatoes (save a 6" piece of tomato peel for garnish) and arrange them all together in a pile on a serving platter. Peel and chop cucumbers and place them next to the tomatoes. Chop green pepper and place next to cucumber. Chop purple onion and place next to pepper. Roll 6" piece of tomato peel into rose shape. Secure with a toothpick and place in the middle of the salad as garnish. In a bowl mix red wine vinegar, tomato sauce, olive oil and lemon juice. Sprinkle with salt and pepper. Spoon vinegar mixture over salad. Top with croutons and serve. Yields 6 servings.

Fun Food Fact: *Today about 10 billion pounds of rice is produced in America. We are the leading rice producers in the world and yet we only produce 2% of the world's rice crop.*

Garden Vegetable Salad

4 medium tomatoes, peeled and cut into wedges
1 small onion, sliced
2 cucumbers, peeled and sliced
1/4 cup commercial Italian dressing

Preparation Time!

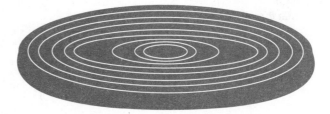

Combine tomatoes, onion and cucumbers. Add dressing and toss gently. Refrigerate until ready to serve. Yields 4 servings.

Fun Food Fact: *Gatorade was developed by Dr. Robert Cade in 1965. His goal was to produce a source of liquids that would replenish the fluids and minerals of his football players...The University of Florida Gators.*

You Are My Sunshine Salad

1 pound carrots, shredded
1 cup sour cream
1 (20-ounce) can crushed pineapple, drained
3/4 cup golden raisins
2 tablespoons honey
3/4 cup flaked coconut
3/4 cup miniature marshmallows.

Combine all ingredients. Toss well and refrigerate. Yields 8 servings.

Fun Food Fact: *The first pretzels were twisted by French monks to resemble the folded arms of someone praying.*

28

Fruity Salad

1 cantaloupe
1 (11-ounce) can mandarine oranges
1 (20-ounce) can pineapple chunks, drained
2-4 fresh peaches, sliced
1 pint fresh strawberries, sliced
1/2 cup sugar
3 tablespoons lemon juice
1/3 cup cranberry juice or orange juice

20 Min.

Preparation Time!

Peel cantaloupe and cut into chunks. Combine remaining ingredients. Chill and serve. Yields 6 servings. This is pretty served in a glass bowl.

Fun Food Fact: Cantaloupe was first grown near Rome, Italy.

Waldorf Salad

2 cups chopped apple
1 cup diced celery
1/3 cup chopped pecans
1/2 cup mayonnaise
Cinnamon

Preparation Time!

Combine apple, celery, nuts and mayonnaise. Toss until everything is well coated. Sprinkle top lightly with cinnamon. Chill. Yields 4 servings.

Fun Food Fact: *In 1896, F. W. Rueckheim and his brother came up with a combination of popcorn, molasses and peanuts. They called their mixture "Cracker Jacks".*

Cranberry Ice

1 (16-ounce) package fresh cranberries
2 cups water
2 cups sugar
1/4 cup lemon juice
1 1/2 teaspoons orange zest (orange rind sliced in thin pieces)
1 1/2 cups water

Preparation Time!

Wash cranberries and place in Microwave safe dish. Add 2 cups water, cover and Microwave on High, stirring every 3 minutes for 15 minutes. Blend mixture well. Stir in sugar, lemon juice, orange zest and cold water. Pour into 9" baking dish. Freeze until firm. Yields 8 servings.

Fun Food Fact: *For over eighty years kids have been unscrewing the two halves of a black and white cookie and eating the middle. Over 200 billion Oreo's have been sold since 1912, when the cookie first made its debut.*

Frozen Fruit Salad

2 cups sour cream
2 tablespoons lemon juice
3/4 cup sugar
1/8 teaspoon salt
1 (8-ounce) can crushed pineapple
1/2 cup chopped cherries
1/4 cup chopped pecans
1 sliced banana
1/2 cup small marshmallows

Preparation Time!

Mix sour cream, juice, sugar and salt. Add remaining ingredients and mix well. Spoon into metal muffin cups and freeze until firm. Remove from cups and serve. Yields 8 servings.

Fun Food Fact: Pine nuts are harvested by hand from wild pine trees in the Southwest and Mexico. They can be ground into flour, eaten raw or roasted. Yes, they do come from the cones of these trees!

Corn Salad

4 ears fresh corn
1/4 cup chopped purple onion
1/4 cup chopped green pepper
1 small peeled and chopped tomato
1 (3 1/4 -ounce) can black olives, sliced
1/4 cup bottled Italian salad dressing
Lettuce leaves

20 Min.

Preparation Time!

Shuck corn and remove silks. Place in a Microwave safe dish with 1/2 cup water. Cover and Microwave on HIGH for 8 minutes. Drain and cool corn. Cut from cob and place in bowl. Add remaining ingredients and toss. Serve on lettuce leaves. Yields 6 servings.

Fun Food Fact: *Potatoes are served in some form or another at 60% of the main meals eaten each day.*

English Pea Salad

1 (17-ounce) can English peas, drained
1 (1-ounce) jar chopped pimentos
1/2 cup American cheese cut into 1/4 inch cubes
1/4 cup mayonnaise

Preparation Time!

Combine all of the ingredients in a bowl and toss until coated with mayonnaise. Chill. Yields 4 servings.

Fun Food Fact: *Moon Pie is a cookie originating from Chattanooga, Tennessee. Very popular in the 1950's, the cookie's daily sales still exceed 300,000 per day.*

Cottage Cheese Salad

1 (16-ounce) container small curd Cottage cheese
3 chopped green onions
2 tablespoons chopped green pepper
2 tablespoons chopped celery
1 small chopped tomato
1/2 teaspoon salt
1/8 teaspoon pepper
Lettuce leaves

Preparation Time!

In a bowl mix cottage cheese, onions, green pepper, celery, tomato, salt and pepper. Toss gently. Refrigerate until ready to serve. Spoon on lettuce leaves and serve.   Yields 4 servings.

Fun Food Fact: Atlanta businessman, Asa G. Chandler, bought the rights to Coca-Cola for $2,300 in 1891 and began marketing the drink as a refreshment. Up to that time Coca-Cola was sold by drug stores for treating headaches and hangovers.

35

Pears on the Half

1 (16-ounce) can pear halves
1 (8-ounce) package cream cheese, softened
1/4 cup honey
1/4 cup vanilla wafer or graham cracker crumbs

20 Min.

Preparation Time!

Drain pear halves and reserve the syrup and set aside. Combine cream cheese and honey. Mix until smooth. Fill each pear half with cream cheese mixture. Sprinkle with crumbs and refrigerate until ready to serve. Yields 6 servings.

Fun Food Fact: Pears originated in Asia. The Bartlett pear is the most common variety grown in America.

Cool Cucumbers

2 cucumbers, sliced
2 small onions, sliced
1/2 teaspoon salt
1/8 teaspoon pepper
1 tablespoon vinegar
1/2 cup sour cream

Preparation Time!

Combine cucumbers, onions, salt, pepper, vinegar and sour cream tossing gently. Cover and chill in refrigerator.
Yields 4 servings.

Fun Food Fact: *Cucumbers are a fruit because the seeds are contained within the flesh of the fruit.*

Asparagus Salad

1 (15-ounce) can asparagus spears
2 sliced tomatoes
1/2 cup crumbled Feta cheese
1/2 cup Italian salad dressing
Lettuce leaves

15 Min.

Preparation Time!

Place 2 tomato slices on lettuce leaf. Arrange 4 asparagus spears on top of tomato. Mix feta cheese and italian salad dressing. Spoon over asparagus. Serve immediately. Yields 6 servings.

Fun Food Fact: *The lollipop was introduced in England in 1780. "Lolly" meant tongue and "pop" referred to the noise made when the lollipop was taken out of the mouth quickly.*

Taco, Taco Salad

1 pound ground beef
1 package taco seasoning
1 head Iceburg lettuce shredded
2 tomatoes, chopped
1 can kidney beans, drained
1 (16-ounce) package tortilla chips
2 green onions, chopped
1 (8-ounce) jar picante sauce
2 cups grated Cheddar cheese
1 (16-ounce) bottle Thousand Island dressing

Preparation Time!

Place ground beef in Microwave safe dish. Cover and Microwave on HIGH, stirring every 3 minutes until done. Add taco seasoning, cover and Microwave for 3 minutes. Combine remaining ingredients and stir in meat. Toss and serve immediately. Yield 10 servings.

Fun Food Fact: *Honey was the first sweetener used widely by man. America has nearly 4 million bee hives producing honey today.*

Layered Tuna Salad

2 (6 1/2-ounce) cans tuna, drained
3/4 cup prepared buttermilk salad dressing
3 chopped green onions
2 cups torn lettuce
2 chopped tomatoes
1 (3.2-ounce) can black olives, drained and sliced
1 avocado, peeled and sliced
1/2 pound bacon, cooked and crumbled

Preparation Time!

Combine tuna and salad dressing, tossing gently. In a serving bowl layer 1 cup lettuce, 1/2 of the tomatoes and 1/2 of the olives and green onion. Spoon half of the tuna mixture over salad. Top with half of sliced avocado and half of bacon. Repeat layering. Yields 6 servings.

Fun Food Fact: *The Kraft food company introduced the "Kraft Dinner" in 1937. Over 300 million boxes of the macaroni and cheese dinner sell every year.*

Stuffed Tomatoes

1 (6 1/2-ounce) can of tuna, drained
3 tablespoons grated carrot
1/2 cup chopped celery
3 green onions, chopped
1 boiled egg, chopped
3/4 cup mayonnaise
4 medium tomatoes
Lettuce
1 (4-ounce) can shoestring potatoes
Paprika

20 Min.

Preparation Time!

In a bowl combine tuna, carrot, celery, green onion, egg and mayonnaise. Toss until mayonnaise covers all ingredients. Wash tomatoes and cut into quarters. Arrange 4 quarters on each lettuce leaf and spoon on tuna mixture. Sprinkle with paprika and top with shoestring potatoes. Yields 4 servings.

Fun Food Fact: RDA is officially known as the "United States Recommended Daily Allowance." This term refers to federal regulations for the minimum amount of nutrients needed by people over the age of 4.

41

Bread Bowls with Broccoli Soup

1 (10 3/4-ounce) can cream of potato soup
1 (10 3/4-ounce) can cream of celery soup
1 1/4 cup milk
1 teaspoon Dijon mustard
1/2 teaspoon dried thyme
1/4 teaspoon basil
1(10-ounce) package frozen broccoli
1/4 cup grated carrot
Grated cheese
4 round loaves of bread (about 6-8" in diameter)

25 Min.

Preparation Time!

Put both cans of soup into a 2-quart saucepan; add milk slowly, stirring until well mixed. Add remaining ingredients and cook over low heat for 40 minutes. Cut the top off of the bread and dig out a bowl-like shape inside. Be careful not to puncture the bottom. Place bread bowl on plate and pour soup inside bowl shape. Garnish with cheese and serve. Eat bowl as well as soup. Yields 4 servings.

Fun Food Fact: *Bread is one of the first foods eaten regularly by man. The art of making bread is over 10,000 years old.*

Garden Potato Soup

Preparation Time!

4 cups peeled and cubed potatoes
1 cup chopped celery
1 cup chopped onion
1/4 cup grated carrot
1/4 cup sliced fresh mushrooms
3 cups water
2 teaspoons salt
1 cup milk
1 cup whipping cream
4 tablespoons butter or margarine
1 tablespoon dried parsley flakes
1/8 teaspoon pepper
grated cheese (optional)

Combine potatoes, celery, onion, carrot, mushrooms, water and salt in large cooking pot. Cover and simmer 20 minutes or until potatoes are tender. Mash mixture with potato masher so that potatoes are mushy. Stir in remaining ingredients, return to heat , simmer for 20 minutes, stirring every two minutes. Top with grated cheese. Yields 6 servings.

Fun Food Fact: Americans eat an everage of three hamburgers per week or more than 38 billion per year.

The Best Vegetable Soup

8 cups water
2 cubes of chicken bouillon
3 medium red potatoes
1 cup elbow macaroni
2 (16-ounce) cans tomatoes, drained and chopped
1/2 cup chopped celery
1/2 cup sliced carrots
1/2 cup chopped onion
1 (10-ounce) package frozen green beans
1 (10-ounce) package frozen corn
1 (10-ounce) package frozen lima beans
1 (10-ounce) package frozen broccoli
1 (10-ounce) package frozen cauliflower
1 tablespoon salt
1/4 teaspoon pepper

Preparation Time!

In a large soup pot, place all of the ingredients listed above. Cover and simmer for 45 minutes or until noodles are tender. Yields 12 servings.

Fun Food Fact: *Jelly beans were first advertised in a Chicago newspaper. They were 9 cents a pound. Not much dough for a lot of beans!*

Chili

Preparation Time!

1 pound ground beef
1 chopped onion
1/4 teaspoon garlic salt
1 (8-ounce) can tomato sauce
1 (8-ounce) can stewed tomatoes
1/4 teaspoon salt
1/8 teaspoon pepper
3 tablespoons chili powder
1 1/2 cups water
Chopped onion
Grated Cheddar cheese
Sour cream

Place ground beef, onion and garlic salt in a Microwave safe dish. Cover and Microwave on HIGH for 9 minutes, stirring every 3 minutes until done. Pour into soup pot or Dutch oven. Add tomato sauce, tomatoes, salt, pepper, chili powder and water. Stir and simmer for 40 minutes. Stir occasionally. Garnish with chopped onion and Cheddar cheese. Serve with sour cream. Yields 4 servings.

Fun Food Fact: In colonial America, rice was grown primarily in South Carolina. During the American Revolution, the British captured the city of Charleston and shipped all of the rice crop to England. In 1787, Thomas Jefferson smuggled some rice seed out of Europe and brought it back to the Carolinas. Rice grows in the Carolinas today.

You'll be Fans of These Potatoes

6 medium baking potatoes
1/4 cup butter or margarine
1/3 cup grated Parmesan cheese
1/2 teaspoon dried parsley flakes
1/4 teaspoon garlic powder
1/4 teaspoon salt
1/8 teaspoon pepper
Paprika

Preparation Time!

Wash potatoes and cut each potato into 1/4 " slices, cutting crosswise almost, but not through, the bottom of the potato. Potatoes will resemble fans. Place potatoes in a bowl of ice water for 5 minutes to open the fans. Drain potatoes and arrange cut side up in a greased 9 x 13 baking dish. Place butter in a Microwave safe dish and cover. Microwave for 1 minute or until melted. Mix cheese, parsley, garlic powder, salt and pepper. Drizzle over potato fans. Sprinkle with paprika and cover dish with foil. Bake at 350° for 40 minutes or until tender.

Fun Food Fact: *The term "organic" refers to any food grown without using chemical fertilizer, pesticides or any other unnatural substances. The FDA regulates the industry and sets standards for what is considered "organic."*

46

Great Corn Pudding

2 cups fresh corn, cut from cob
1/4 cup flour
1 tablespoon sugar
1 teaspoon salt
2 cups milk
2 eggs, beaten
2 tablespoons butter or margarine

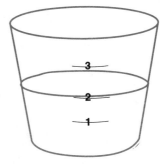

20 Min.

Preparation Time!

Combine corn, flour, sugar, and salt. Gradually add milk and blend eggs and butter into mixture. Pour into greased 9 X 9 baking dish. Bake at 350° for 1 hour. Stir every ten minutes for the first 30 minutes. Yields 6 servings.

Fun Food Fact: *The substitute for chocolate is carob. It comes from the pods grown on the carob tree.*

Confetti Broccoli

2 pounds fresh broccoli
1/2 cup sliced green onion
1/4 cup water
2 tablespoons butter or margarine
2 tablespoons chopped pimento
1 teaspoon grated lemon rind
2 tablespoons lemon juice
1 teaspoon salt
1/8 teaspoon pepper

Preparation Time!

Trim broccoli and wash, cut into medium pieces. Place broccoli in Microwave safe dish with 1/4 cup water. Cover and Microwave on HIGH for 4 minutes. Carefully remove broccoli, drain and place in serving dish. Place the onion and butter in Microwave safe dish and Microwave on HIGH for 1 minute. Add the remaining ingredients and pour over the broccoli. 6 servings.

Fun Food Fact: *Grenadine is a sweet syrup with a deep red color made from pomegranates. It is used in the popular cocktail, Shirley Temple, a kid's specialty drink.*

Zesty Corn on the Cob

1/2 cup butter or margarine, softened
4 tablespoons chopped fresh parsley
4 tablespoons chopped fresh chives
1 teaspoon dry buttermilk salad dressing mix
1/8 teaspoon pepper
8 ears of fresh corn

15 Min.

Preparation Time!

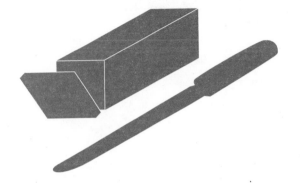

Combine butter, parsley, chives, dry salad dressing mix and pepper. Mix well and set aside. Remove husks and silks from corn. Place ears in Microwave safe dish with 1/4 cup water. Cover and Microwave on HIGH for 4 minutes, turning the dish one quarter turn. Microwave on HIGH for another 4 minutes or until kernels pop easily when poked with a fork. Drain well. Spread the butter mixture over hot corn and serve. Yields 8 servings.

Fun Food Fact: Cayenne pepper is a seasoning used in many recipes. It is made with ground chile peppers and salt.

Heavenly Potatoes

1 (32-ounce) package frozen hash brown potatoes, thawed
3/4 cup butter or margarine melted
1/2 cup chopped onion
1 can cream of mushroom soup
1 cup sour cream
1 cup grated Cheddar cheese
2 cups corn flakes
1 tablespoon Parsley flakes
1/8 teaspoon pepper

Preparation Time!

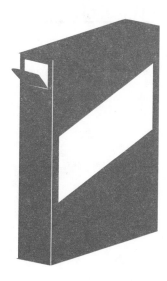

Combine potatoes, 1/2 cup butter, onion, soup, sour cream and cheese, stir well. Spoon into greased 9 x 13 baking dish. Crush cereal and stir in remaining butter. Sprinkle over potato mixture. Bake at 350° for 50 minutes. Yields 10 servings.

Fun Food Fact: *Food grown in water is called Aquaculture. Currently more than 3000 farms in America produce 15% of our supply of seafood.*

Festive Corn

2 tablespoons butter or margarine
1/4 cup chopped green pepper
2 (12-ounce) cans corn, drained
3 tablespoons chopped pimento
1/8 teaspoon salt

15 Min.

Preparation Time!

Combine butter and green pepper in a Microwave safe dish. Cover and Microwave on HIGH for 2 minutes. Stir in corn, pimento and salt. Cover and Microwave on HIGH for 4 minutes stirring every 2 minutes until mixture is thoroughly heated. Yields 6 servings.

Fun Food Fact: *The name hamburger comes from the German city of Hamburg. It appeared first in America as a menu item in 1834 in a New York restaurant named Delmonicos.*

Buttercup New Potatoes

18 small new potatoes
1/2 cup water
2 tablespoons butter or margarine
2 tablespoons all-purpose flour
1/4 teaspoon dry mustard
1 1/4 cups milk
1/2 cup Cheddar cheese, grated
2 tablespoons fresh parsley
2 tablespoons fresh chives
1/2 teaspoon salt

25 Min.

Preparation Time!

Wash potatoes; peel a 1/2" strip around the center of each potato. Place potatoes in Microwave safe dish. Add 1/2 cup water, cover and Microwave on HIGH stirring potatoes every 3 minutes until tender. Drain and set aside. Place butter in a Microwave safe dish and cover. Melt butter on HIGH for 1 minute or until melted. Add flour and mustard, mix well. Cook in Microwave for 1 minute. Gradually add milk, stirring constantly. Cover and Microwave until thickened, stirring every 2 minutes. Add remaining ingredients and and stir until cheese melts. Pour over potatoes and serve.

Fun Food Fact: *The design of the egg is very durable. It remains one of the most delicate breakable materials; yet pressure can be distributed evenly all over and it won't break.*

EZ Gourmet Broccoli

2 pounds fresh broccoli
1/4 cup water
1/3 cup butter or margarine
4-6 teaspoons capers, undrained

15 Min.

Preparation Time!

Wash and cut broccoli up into pieces. Place in Microwave safe dish with 1/4 cup water. Cover and Microwave on HIGH for 8 minutes, stirring every 2 minutes until tender. Drain and place in serving dish. Place butter in Microwave safe dish. Cover and Microwave for 1 minute or until melted. Add capers to butter and spoon sauce over broccoli. Yields 6 servings.

Fun Food Fact: *Almonds were introduced in California in the mid 1800's. California now produces more than half of the world's crop.*

Fresh Spinach

1 pound fresh spinach
4 tablespoons water
1/4 cup butter or margarine
1 medium onion, chopped
1/2 cup sour cream
1/4 teaspoon salt
1/8 teaspoon pepper
Paprika

Remove stems from spinach; wash leaves thoroughly and tear into pieces. Place in Microwave safe dish. Add 4 tablespoons water. Cover dish with plastic wrap and Microwave for 5 minutes on HIGH or until tender. Carefully remove plastic, drain off water and place spinach on paper towels and squeeze all remaining water out of spinach. Heat onions and butter in Microwave until onions are tender. Add drained spinach to onions and butter, add sour cream, salt and pepper and toss gently. Sprinkle with paprika and Microwave until throughly heated. Yields 4 servings.

Fun Food Fact: *In 1927 Daniel Gerber began marketing baby food under his own name. Until Gerber, mothers made their own baby food from mashed foods.*

Oven Fries

4 large red potatoes
3 tablespoons olive oil
1/2 teaspoon thyme
1/2 teaspoon chopped parsley
1 teaspoon salt
1/4 teaspoon pepper
1/8 teaspoon paprika

15 Min.

Preparation Time!

Wash and scrub potatoes. Cut into strips about 1/2" thick. Place cut potatoes in cold water until ready to use. Drain potatoes and dry on paper towels. Mix olive oil with the remaining ingredients and toss with potatoes. Spread potatoes out on cookie sheet. Bake at 425° for 35 minutes, turning occasionally with spatula until potatoes are crisp on all sides. Be sure to wear oven mitts. Yields 6 servings.

Fun Food Fact: Out of all the billions of gallons of milk produced in America each year here is how we use it all: 37.3% sold as fresh milk or cream, 32% goes to make cheese, 17% goes in butter, 8.3% is used in frozen desserts or dessert topping, 1.3 % is used as condensed or evaporated milk.

Honey Orange Carrots

1 pound carrots
3/4 cup water
1/2 teaspoon salt
1/2 teaspoon grated orange peel
1 orange
2 tablespoons butter or margarine
3 tablespoons honey

20 Min.

Preparation Time!

Wash and scrape carrots. Slice into rounds and place in Microwave safe dish. Add water. Cover and Microwave on HIGH for 15 minutes, stirring every 5 minutes until carrots are tender. Drain carrots and add orange peel. Peel orange and chop into small pieces. Add to carrots with butter and honey. Stir to mix ingredients. Cover and Microwave on HIGH for 2 minutes. Serve. Yields 6 servings.

Fun Food Fact: In colonial America the pumpkin was so plentiful and grew so easily that the colonists made beer, soup and bread out of pumpkin. They were frugal and even roasted the seeds to be eaten as a snack.

Mexican Ole' Rice

2 cups uncooked regular rice
3 cups chicken broth
1/2 cup water
3 tablespoon butter or margarine
1 (10-ounce) can diced chilies and tomatoes, drained
2 cups sour cream
2 1/2 cups shredded Monterey Jack cheese
Paprika

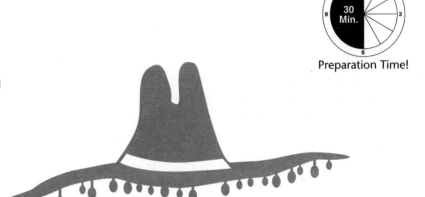

30 Min.

Preparation Time!

Combine first four ingredients in a Microwave safe dish. Cover and Microwave on HIGH for 20 minutes, stirring every 5 minutes until done. Stir drained can of diced chilies and tomatoes into rice, add sour cream and cheese. Spoon mixture into greased 9 x 13 cooking dish and top with paprika. Cover with foil and bake for 30 minutes at 350°. Yields 8 servings.

Fun Food Fact: *Americans average rice consumption per year is 20 pounds.*

Broccoli and Cheese Casserole

1 (10-ounce) package frozen chopped broccoli
1 large onion, chopped
5 tablespoons water
1/2 cup butter or margarine
1 1/3 cup rice, cooked
1 (8-ounce) jar of process cheese spread
1 can cream of mushroom soup

Preparation Time!

Place broccoli and onion in Microwave safe bowl, add 5 tablespoons water. Cover with plastic and Microwave for 8 minutes on HIGH, stirring every 2 minutes. Be careful about lifting the plastic to stir. Let the steam escape. Drain off excess water. Add remaining ingredients and mix well. Pour into greased 9 x 13 baking dish and bake at 350° for 30 minutes. Yields 8 servings.

Fun Food Fact: *Cheese is a food made from the pressed curd of milk.*

Gotcha Green Beans

1 (16-ounce) can of whole green beans
1 purple onion
1/4 cup water
3/4 cup red wine vinegar
1/2 cup salad oil
1/4 teaspoon garlic powder
1 teaspoon sugar
1 teaspoon dill
1/2 teaspoon dry mustard
1/4 teaspoon salt

Preparation Time!

Drain green beans and place in bowl. Slice onion and separate into rings. Place over green beans. Mix remaining ingredients and pour over green beans and onions. Toss gently to distribute liquids evenly. These beans can be served warm or cold. Yields 4 servings.

Fun Food Fact: Native Americans believed that angry demons lived in popcorn and that they exploded when exposed to heat.

5 Star Tomatoes

4 medium tomatoes
1/2 cup breadcrumbs
1/4 cup Parmesan cheese
1 tablespoon butter or margarine, melted
1/8 teaspoon salt
1/8 teaspoon pepper
1/8 teaspoon garlic powder
1 teaspoon parsley leaves

Preparation Time!

Cut tomatoes in half. Mix the remaining ingredients. Press the top of the tomatoes into the breadcrumb mixture. Place tomatoes crumb side up in greased 9 x 13 baking dish. Bake at 350° for 20 minutes. Yields 8 servings.

Fun Food Fact: *Cooking wines are added to food for the flavor. The alcohol in the wine is burned off during the cooking or heating process leaving only the taste.*

Baked Squash

4 cups fresh yellow crookneck squash
1 chopped onion
3 tablespoons butter or margarine
1 teaspoon salt
1/8 teaspoon pepper
1 cup evaporated milk
2 cups bread crumbs
1 egg, beaten
1 cup Parmesan cheese, divided

20 Min.

Preparation Time!

Wash squash and cut into slices. Place in Microwave safe dish with onion, butter, salt and pepper. Cover and Microwave on High for 8 minutes, stirring every 4 minutes or until done. Add cracker crumbs, milk, egg and half of the Parmesan cheese. Mix well and pour into greased 9 x 9 baking dish. Top with remaining cheese. Bake at 350° for 30 minutes. Yields 6 servings.

Fun Food Fact: *Espresso is a dark, bitter coffee. It originated in Italy. The word espresso means to "press out" and that is what happens in an espresso machine. The coffee is pressed out of the bean using pressure and steam.*

Cheesy Potato Sticks

4 large red potatoes
4 tablespoons butter or margarine, melted
1/4 teaspoon seasoned salt
1/8 teaspoon onion salt
1/8 teaspoon paprika
1/2 teaspoon parsley
1/4 cup Parmesan cheese

Preparation Time!

Scrub potatoes and cut into 1/4" strips. Place in a bowl of ice water for 10 minutes. Drain off water and pat dry on paper towels. Toss gently with butter. Mix seasoned salt, onion salt, paprika, parsley and Parmesan cheese. Sprinkle mixture over potatoes and toss again. Spread potatoes on cookie sheet and bake at 400° for 30 minutes, turning occasionally with spatula. Remember to wear oven mitts when turning potatoes. Yields 6 servings.

Fun Food Fact: "Hoppin John" is a southern dish of cowpeas and rice. It is served on New Year's Day to ensure that the eater will have "good luck" during the following year.

Fresh Vegetables

1 cup fresh carrots
3 tablespoons water
1/4 teaspoon salt
1 tablespoon butter or margarine
1 cup fresh cauliflower
1 cup fresh broccoli
3 tablespoons lemon juice
1 tablespoon butter or margarine

20 Min.

Preparation Time!

Scrape carrots and cut into slices. Place in Microwave safe dish with water, salt and butter. Cover and Microwave on HIGH for 3 minutes. Cut cauliflower and broccoli into chunks and add to carrots. Microwave on HIGH for 9 minutes, stirring every three minutes until done. Add lemon juice and butter to hot veggies and toss. Serve. Yields 4 servings.

Fun Food Fact: *The first supermarket opened in 1916. It was owned and designed by Clarence Saunders of Memphis, Tennessee. He designed the store so that customers could choose their items from shelves. Before Clarence's Piggly Wiggly stores customers were waited on individually, one at a time. They told the merchant what they wanted and he collected the items and brought them up to the front of the store. There were no "Express" lanes.*

Rice Patties

1 cup uncooked rice
2 1/2 cups water
2 tablespoons butter or margarine
1 cup grated Cheddar cheese
1/3 cup chopped onion
1/3 cup chopped celery
2 tablespoons chopped red pepper
1 teaspoon salt
3 eggs, beaten
1 1/2 cups milk
1 tablespoon chopped parsley

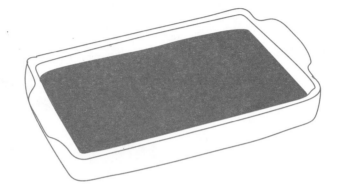

Preparation Time!

Place rice and butter in Microwave safe dish and add 2 1/2 cups water. Cover and Microwave on HIGH for 20 minutes, stirring every 5 minutes until done. Mix rice, cheese, onion, celery and red pepper. Add salt, eggs and milk. Mix well and pour into greased 9 x 13 baking dish. Sprinkle top with parsley and bake at 350° for 45 minutes. Cut into squares and serve. Yields 8 servings.

Fun Food Fact: Captain James Cook introduced the pineapple to the Hawaiian islands in 1790. Only when transportation from the islands to the mainland was regular and dependable, did the pineapple become economically important as a crop.

64

Italian Zucchini

4 small zucchini, sliced
2 tablespoons butter or margarine
1 large tomato, peeled and chopped
1 small onion, thinly sliced
1/2 teaspoon salt
1/8 teaspoon pepper
1/4 cup Italian salad dressing

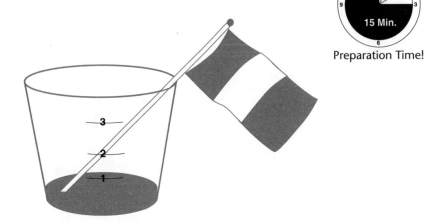

15 Min.

Preparation Time!

Place zucchini in Microwave safe dish, cover with plastic and Microwave on HIGH for 3 minutes. Add remaining ingredients and stir gently. Cover and Microwave on HIGH for 4 more minutes or until all vegetables are tender. Yield 4 servings.

Fun Food Fact: *Americans eat an average of 270 eggs per person each year.*

Spring Potatoes

10 - 12 new potatoes
1 teaspoon sugar
1 teaspoon salt
1/2 teaspoon parsley
1/4 teaspoon garlic powder
1/4 cup butter or margarine
2 tablespoons lemon juice
Paprika

20 Min.

Preparation Time!

Wash potatoes and peel off a strip of peeling around the middle of each potato to make them look prettier. Place potatoes, sugar, salt, parsley and garlic powder in a large Microwave safe bowl. Cover potatoes with water and cover bowl with plastic. Microwave on HIGH for 8 minutes. Carefully remove plastic and stir potatoes around to distribute heat evenly. Recover and Microwave on HIGH for 8 more minutes or until potatoes are tender. Drain and place potatoes in serving dish. Combine butter and lemon juice. Cover and melt in Microwave on HIGH for 1 minute. Drizzle butter over potatoes and sprinkle with paprika. Toss gently. Yields 6 servings.

Fun Food Fact: *Christopher Columbus discovered that the Indians of the New World were using chili peppers that they grew themselves to flavor their food. The Aztecs put chili peppers in everything, even chocolate. This gives new meaning to "Hot Chocolate"!*

66

Rice Pilaf

3/4 cup sliced green onions
2 tablespoons butter or margarine
1 cup uncooked rice
1/2 cup chopped green pepper
2 tablespoons chopped fresh parsley
2 cups chicken broth
1/2 cup water
1/2 teaspoon salt
1/8 teaspoon pepper

20 Min.

Preparation Time!

Place onions and butter in Microwave safe dish. Cover and Microwave on HIGH for 2 minutes. Add rice, green pepper, parsley, chicken broth, water, salt and pepper. Cover and Microwave on HIGH, stirring every 3 minutes until rice is tender and liquid is absorbed. Yields 6 servings.

Fun Food Fact: Chile peppers are graded from 0-300,000 in Scoville Units. This measurement determines how HOT the chile peppers taste. The measurements were first done by humans (a really hot job.) Now they are tested by "High Pressure Liquid Chromotography." For a reference point, the Jalapeno pepper measures from 2500-5000 Scoville Units.

67

Potatoes Anna

1/2 cup melted butter or margarine
2 pounds new potatoes, scrubbed and peeled
1/2 teaspoon chopped fresh parsley
Salt
Pepper

Preparation Time!

Coat a nonstick 9" cakepan with butter. Cut potatoes crosswise into 1/8" thick slices. Starting in the center of the pan, arrange a thin layer of potato slices, overlapping, on the bottom of the cakepan. Drizzle 2 tablespoons of the butter over the top of the potatoes and salt and pepper them lightly. Repeat layering of potatoes, butter and salt and pepper. Place a piece of buttered foil on the top of the potatoes. Place another pan on top of the foil to compact the potatoes (anything heavy and ovenproof would work). Bake covered at 400° for 40 minutes. Remove pan on top and the foil and bake for 20 more minutes uncovered. Drain off excess butter and invert potatoes onto a serving platter. Garnish with parsley and serve. Yields 6 servings.

Fun Food Fact: *Chocolate and cocoa come from the bean "Theobroma cacao". The bean was believed to have been brought by the gods. The cacao beans were very valuable and used as currency in parts of Mexico. Now you know why they say "that will cost a few beans".*

Holiday Green Beans

1 (10 3/4-ounce) can of cream of mushroom soup
1/2 cup milk
1 teaspoon soy sauce
1/8 teaspoon pepper
2 (15-ounce) cans cut green beans, drained
1 (3 1/2-ounce) can french fried onions

15 Min.

Preparation Time!

In a bowl mix soup, milk, soy sauce and pepper. Add drained green beans and 1/2 can of french fried onions. Mix and pour into greased 9 x 13 baking dish. Sprinkle remaining 1/2 can of french fried onions on top. Bake uncovered at 350° for 30 minutes. Yields 6 servings.

Fun Food Fact: *Shrimp is the most popular shellfish in America. We harvest over 370 million pounds every year. In addition to all the shrimp we harvest, we import an additional 200 million pounds to meet the demand.*

Zuc-ca (Zucchini and Carrots)

4 medium carrots
3 tablespoons water
2 medium zucchini
3 tablespoons butter or margarine, melted
1/4 teaspoon salt
1/8 teaspoon pepper
2 tablespoons chopped fresh parsley

15 Min.

Preparation Time!

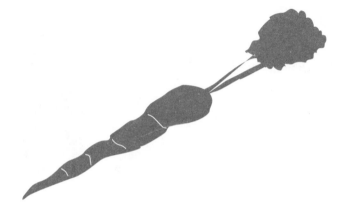

Wash and scrape carrots and cut into 1/4" thick pieces. Cut zucchini into thin strips. Place carrots in a Microwave safe dish with 3 tablespoons water and Microwave for 4 minutes. Drain off excess water and add zucchini, butter, salt, pepper and parsley. Cover and Microwave until carrots are tender. Yields 6 servings.

Fun Food Fact: Peanut butter is a favorite food of Americans. We eat over 3.36 pounds each year.

Spiced Cooked Apples

3 tart apples
1/2 cup brown sugar, packed
1 teaspoon lemon juice
1/4 teaspoon cinnamon
2 tablespoons butter or margarine, melted
1 tablespoon all-purpose flour

Preparation Time!

Core and slice apples. Combine apples, sugar, lemon juice, cinnamon, butter and flour. Toss gently until apples are well coated. Spoon into greased 9 x 9 baking dish. Cover with foil and bake at 350° for 30 minutes. Serve over vanilla ice cream or as a side dish to pork, ham or chicken. Yields 4 servings.

Fun Food Fact: *The ancient Egyptians were some of the first people to have candy. They preserved nuts and fruit with honey. Caramels were some of the next candies known to man and they appeared in the early 1700's. Today Americans consume over 20 pounds of candy per person each year.*

Baked Potato Bar

4 large baking potatoes
8 tablespoons butter or margarine
1/2 cup grated Cheddar cheese
3 chopped green onions
6 slices bacon cooked and crumbled
1/2 cup sour cream
Use your imagination!

Preparation Time!

Wash and scrub potatoes and bake at 350° for 50 minutes or until tender. Remove potatoes from oven with oven mitts or hot pads. On a platter place in separate sections the cheese, onion, bacon and any other fresh vegetables on hand. Place butter and sour cream in separate bowls. Let each person make their own potato creation. Other suggestions include green pepper, broccoli, salsa. The list is endless. Yields 4 servings.

Fun Food Fact: *Even heard of a Progressive Dinner? It is a dinner in which each course of the meal is eaten at a different neighbor's house.*

Fresh Pasta

1/3 cup milk
3 tablespoons butter or margarine
1/4 teaspoon salt
1 (7-ounce) package of vermicelli
1/4 cup lemon juice
1/3 cup grated Parmesan cheese
1 teaspoon chopped fresh parsley
Lemon zest (6-8 thin slices of lemon rind)

Preparation Time!

Combine milk and butter in Microwave safe dish. Microwave on HIGH for 1 minute or until butter is melted. Place vermicelli and salt in Microwave safe dish and cover with water. Microwave on HIGH, stirring every 2 minutes, until vermicelli is tender. Drain and add lemon juice tossing gently to coat the vermicelli. Add cheese to milk mixture and pour over vermicelli. Toss gently and sprinkle parsley on top and add zest. Yields 6 servings.

Fun Food Fact: *The first licensed character to be put on a lunch box was Mickey Mouse, but the lunch box boom really began in 1950 when Aladdin Industries in Nashville put Hopalong Cassidy on a lunch box. The company sold over 500,000 lunch boxes with this TV cowboy hero featured on the front.*

Romanoff Noodles

1 (8-ounce) package of egg noodles
1 (8-ounce) carton sour cream
1/2 cup grated Parmesan cheese, divided
1 tablespoon chopped fresh chives
1 teaspoon salt
1/8 teaspoon pepper
1/4 teaspoon garlic powder
2 tablespoons butter or margarine

Preparation Time!

Place noodles in Microwave safe dish, cover with water. Cover dish and Microwave on HIGH, stirring every 3 minutes until noodles are tender. Drain and stir in butter. Mix sour cream, 1/2 of cheese, chives, salt, pepper, garlic powder. Pour mixture over noodles and toss. Sprinkle top with remaining cheese. Yields 6 servings.

Fun Food Fact: *In the 1890's George Washington Carver promoted the peanut as a replacement crop for cotton. The cotton crops were destroyed by the boll weevil. Since then hundreds of uses for peanuts have been found, demonstrating its highly nutritive value.*

74

Macaroni and Cheese

1 (8-ounce) package elbow macaroni
1/4 cup butter or margarine
3 tablespoons all-purpose flour
2 cups milk
1 teaspoon salt
2 cups grated Cheddar cheese
1 egg, beaten
Paprika

35 Min.

Preparation Time!

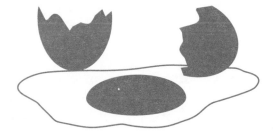

Place macaroni noodles in Microwave safe dish and add 3 cups water. Cover and Microwave on HIGH for 18 minutes, stirring every 3 minutes until noodles are tender. Drain and set aside. Place margarine in Microwave safe dish and Microwave on High for 1 minute or until butter is melted. Add flour and salt and stir until smooth. Pour milk in flour mixture gradually, stirring constantly. Add egg and mix again. Microwave on HIGH for 6 minutes, stirring every 3 minutes until mixture thickens. Add cheese and stir until melted. Stir cheese mixture into macaroni and pour into 9 x 13 baking dish. Sprinkle with paprika and bake at 350° for 35 minutes.

Fun Food Fact: *Ever heard of "redeye gravy" and wonder what it is? It's a southern tradition and is made from pan drippings after frying ham. In most recipes it is flavored with coffee.*

Souffle with Cheese

4 slices of bread
1 cup grated Sharp Cheddar cheese
3 eggs
1 cup milk
1 teaspoon dry mustard
1/2 teaspoon salt
1/8 teaspoon pepper

Preparation Time!

Tear slices of bread into small pieces and place on the bottom of a greased 9 x 9 baking dish. Sprinkle bread with cheese. Beat eggs with a wire wisk and add milk, mustard, salt and pepper. Mix well and pour over cheese. Bake at 425° for 20 minutes or until top is light brown. Yields 4 servings.

Fun Food Fact: *An eleven year old boy named Frank Eperson invented the "popsicle" in 1905 when he left a mixing stick in a glass of juice on the window sill. The juice froze with the stick in it. Kids can do the most amazing things!*

Camp Fire Chicken

2 chickens (halfed)
4 small onions, sliced
1 cup sliced carrots
1 cup sliced potatoes
4 tablespoons butter or margarine
2 tablespoons parsley
4 slices lemon
Salt
Pepper

20 Min.

Preparation Time!

Salad Page 27
Dessert Page 114
Set the table Page 125

Cut 4 large pieces of aluminum foil. Place half of each chicken on foil. Add sliced onion. Divide carrots and potatoes evenly between the four chicken halves. Top each with a tablespoon of butter, 1/2 teaspoon parsley and slice of lemon. Salt and pepper generously. Bring sides of foil up around chicken and fold over, making a secure seal. Bring in the ends and seal again. Be sure that seals are on the top of chicken package so that the fluids and steam will remain trapped inside for basting chicken. Bake at 350° for 50 minutes or until done. Be careful unwrapping chicken, avoiding steam. This can be cooked in the oven or on the grill. This recipe is great for camp fires too!

Fun Food Fact: In 1802 Thomas Moore built the ice box. It was a free standing insulated chest and housed a 100 pound block of ice that kept food cold.

Upside Down Pizza

1 pound ground beef
1 chopped onion
1/2 tablespoon chopped parsley
1 (1.5-ounce) package spaghetti sauce mix
1 (15-ounce) can tomato sauce
2 cups grated Mozzarella cheese
2 eggs
1 cup milk
1 tablespoon vegetable oil
1 cup all-purpose flour
1/4 teaspoon salt
1/2 cup grated Parmesan cheese
Paprika

Preparation Time!

Salad Page 24
Dessert Page 123
Set the table Page 125

Place ground beef and chopped onion in Microwave safe dish. Cover and Microwave on HIGH for 9 minutes, stirring every 3 minutes until done. Add parsley, spaghetti sauce mix, tomato sauce and mix. Cover and Microwave on HIGH for 3 minutes. Spoon mixture into greased 9 x 13 baking dish. Top with Mozzarella cheese. In a bowl, beat eggs and oil until foamy. Add flour and salt and beat until smooth. Pour over cheese and meat and spread evenly. Sprinkle the top with Parmesan cheese and paprika. Bake uncovered at 400° for 30 minutes or until top is golden brown. Cut into squares and serve. Yields 8 servings.

Fun Food Fact: *The raisin industry began in California in 1873 when a heat wave hit the area and dried out most of the grape harvest. One creative business man in San Francisco began marketing the dried harvest as "Peruvian Delicacies." That's marketing!*

Pasta Carbonera

1 (12-ounce) package spaghetti
3 eggs, beaten
1 cup grated Parmesan cheese, divided
1/2 cup whipping cream
10 slices bacon, cooked and crumbled
1/4 cup chopped fresh parsley
1/4 teaspoon dried basil
1/4 cup butter or margarine
1/4 teaspoon garlic salt

25 Min.

Preparation Time!

Salad Page 29
Vegetable Page 60
Dessert Page 100
Set the table Page 125

Break spaghetti into three sections and place in Microwave safe dish. Cover with water and Microwave on HIGH for 20 minutes, stirring every 4 minutes. Drain and add bacon, parsley, basil. Toss and set aside, keeping warm. Combine eggs and 1/2 cup cheese, stirring well. Heat whipping cream in Microwave on High for 2 minutes. Add butter and egg and cheese mixture. Cover and Microwave until butter is melted. Pour over spaghetti mixture and toss again. Top with remaining 1/2 cup Parmesan cheese. Serve immediately. Yields 6 servings.

Fun Food Fact: *NutraSweet is aspartic acid and phenylalanine. It was created by accident in 1965 by chemist James M. Schlatter while working for G. D. Searle and Company in Illinois.*

Easy Enchiladas

1 1/2 pounds ground beef
1 chopped onion
1 (1.5-ounce) envelope taco seasoning mix
1 (10-ounce) can diced tomatoes and chilies
1 (10 3/4-ounce) can cream of mushroom soup
1 (12-ounce) bag of plain tortilla chips
2 cups grated American cheese
Sour cream

20 Min.

Preparation Time!

Salad Page 26
Dessert Page 117
Set the table Page 125

Place ground beef and onion in Microwave safe container. Cover and Microwave on HIGH for 9 minutes, stirring beef mixture every 3 minutes or until done. Drain mixture. Add taco seasoning mix, can of diced tomatoes and chilies and soup. Mix well. In a greased 9 x 13 baking dish, layer about 1/3 of the beef mixture. Top with broken tortilla chips and 1/3 of cheese. Repeat layering until all of beef mixture is used. Cover and bake at 350° for 30 minutes. Serve with sour cream. Yields 6 servings.

Fun Food Fact: The name for the "hush puppy" came from cooks throwing them to the dogs and yelling "hush, puppies."

Swiss Steak

2 pounds round steak
Salt
Pepper
2 tablespoons butter or margarine
1/4 cup chopped onion
1/4 cup chopped green pepper
1/4 cup chopped celery
1 (15-ounce) can stewed tomatoes
2 tablespoons flour
1 cup hot water

Preparation Time!

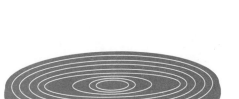

Salad Page 28
Vegetable Page 68
Dessert Page 119
Set the table Page 125

Wash steak and cut into serving size pieces, dust both sides lightly with salt and pepper. Place in greased 9 x 13 baking dish. Place butter, onion, green pepper and celery in Microwave safe dish and Microwave on HIGH for 3 minutes. Mix with can of stewed tomatoes and pour over steak. Cover and bake at 350° for 45 minutes or until steak is done. Mix flour with hot water and pour over steak. If flour and water mixture is lumpy, pour over steak through a strainer. Move pieces of steak around mixing flour mixture with other juices. Cover again and bake for 5 more minutes. Serve. Yields 6 servings. Be careful because the dish is HOT!

Fun Food Fact: The fruit of the prickly pear cactus can be eaten. It is removed from the cactus and eaten in salads or made into jams and jellies.

Chicken Italiano

2 cups Italian breadcrumbs
1/2 cup grated Parmesan cheese
1 teaspoon garlic salt
1/2 teaspoon pepper
4 -6 skinless chicken breasts
1/2 cup butter or margarine, melted

20 Min.

Preparation Time!

Salad Page 30
Vegetable Page 49
Dessert Page 115
Set the table Page 125

Combine breadcrumbs, cheese, salt and pepper. Dip chicken in butter. Coat chicken by dipping and rolling in crumb mixture. Place in greased 9 x 13 baking dish; sprinkle remaining breading mixture over chicken breasts. Bake at 350° for 45 minutes or until done. Yields 4-6 servings.

Fun Food Fact: *"Free range" chickens are allowed to forage for food on their own and are not penned up all day. This type of chicken production is reported to produce healthier chickens for consumption.*

82

Mexicali Chicken

25 Min.

Preparation Time!

1 (10 3/4-ounce) can cream of chicken soup
1 (10-ounce) can diced tomatoes and green chilies
1/4 cup chopped onion
1 bag corn chips
2 cups cooked chopped chicken
1 1/2 cups grated Cheddar Cheese

Salad Page 24
Dessert Page 118
Set the table Page 125

In a bowl combine soup, tomatoes and green chilies, and onion. In a greased 9 x 13 baking dish layer corn chips, half of the soup mixture, the chicken and cheese. Repeat layer and top with cheese. Cover and bake at 350° for 30 minutes. Yields 6 servings.

Fun Food Fact: *The cashew nut comes from the end of an apple from the Cashew tree. The evergreen tree grows in tropical regions in the Americas.*

Make Ahead Easy Lasagna

1 1/2 pound ground beef
1 chopped onion
1 (30 -ounce) jar garden vegetable spaghetti sauce
1 (8-ounce) carton small curd cottage cheese
1/2 cup water
1 box lasagna noodles, uncooked
1 (12-ounce) package sliced Mozzarella cheese

Preparation Time!

Salad Page 26
Dessert Page 122
Set the table Page 125

Place ground beef and onion in Microwave safe dish. Cover and Microwave on HIGH for 9 minutes, stirring every 3 minutes. Add spaghetti sauce and cottage cheese. Mix well. Layer some of beef mixture on bottom of 9 x 13 baking dish. Place 3 lasagna noodles on top of beef. Top with another layer of beef mixture and 3 slices of cheese. Add 3 more lasagna noodles and more beef mixture. Top with 3 slices of cheese. Repeat layering until all of beef mixture is used. Top with 3 slices of cheese. Pour 1/2 cup water around the sides of dish. Cover with foil and refrigerate until ready to bake. Remove dish from refrigerator and place in cold oven. Set oven at 350° and bake for 45 minutes or until hot throughout.

Fun Food Fact: *Many pyrex serving containers need to make temperature changes gradually. That is why we recommend that they go from refrigerator to a cold oven, instead of a preheated oven.*

Pork Chops, Pork Chops, Easy, Easy

1 cup cracker crumbs
1/4 cup Parmesan cheese
1 tablespoon parsley flakes
1 teaspoon salt
1/8 teaspoon pepper
6 pork chops (chicken can be substituted)
1/2 cup butter or margarine, melted

15 Min.

Preparation Time!

Salad Page 34
Vegetable Page 46
Dessert Page 124
Set the table Page 125

Combine cracker crumbs, cheese, parsley, salt, and pepper. Dip pork chops into melted butter and coat with crumb mixture. Place in greased 9 x 13 baking dish. Top with remaining crumb mixture. Bake at 350° for 1 hour or until done. Yields 6 servings.

Fun Food Fact: $300 million dollars in Girl Scout Cookies are sold in America each year. The most popular variety is "Thin Mints."

Pizza Meat Loaf

Preparation Time!

2 lbs ground beef
2 eggs, beaten
2 tablespoons chopped onion
2 tablespoons chopped green pepper
3/4 cup bread crumbs
1/2 cup tomato juice
2 teaspoons parsley
1/2 teaspoon oregano
1/4 teaspoon salt
1/4 teaspoon pepper
1 small clove garlic
8 slices boiled ham
8 slices mozzarella cheese, reserve one slice for top

Salad Page 36
Vegetable Page 47
Dessert Page 116
Set the table Page 125

Blend ground beef and the next 10 ingredients. Mix well and roll out on wax paper to about 1" thick. Lay sliced ham on top of beef and cheese on top of ham. Roll meat loaf up like a jelly roll. Pinch ends closed and place in pan. Bake at 350° for about 65 minutes. Add one slice of cheese to top and serve. Yields 12 servings.

Fun Food Fact: *Allspice comes from the dried berry on the pimento bush that grows in Central America and the West Indies. The name came from the taste of the berry. It tastes like a mixture of cinnamon, cloves and nutmeg. That is why it is called Allspice.*

Chili Dogs

8 hot dog buns
Spicy Brown mustard
1 (15-ounce) can chili with beans
8 frankfurters
1 cup grated American cheese
1/2 cup chopped onion

Preparation Time!

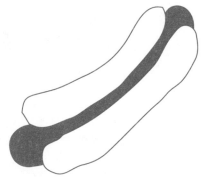

Vegetable Page 49
Dessert Page 118
Set the table Page 125

Place chili in a Microwave safe dish, cover and heat thoroughly. Place frankfurters on Microwave safe dish and poke with fork several times. Microwave on HIGH for 3 minutes. Place frankfurters on buns , spoon chili on frankfurters and top with grated cheese and onion.

Fun Food Fact: The average person eats 80 hot dogs per year.

Tostada Dinners

1 pound ground beef
1/2 cup chopped onion
1/2 teaspoon chili powder
1/2 teaspoon salt
1 (8 1/2-ounce) can kidney beans
6 corn tostadas
1 large tomato, chopped
3 cups shredded lettuce
1 avocado, peeled and cut into pieces
1 cup Cheddar cheese
Taco sauce
Sour cream

25 Min.

Preparation Time!

Dessert Page 86
Set the table Page 125

Combine ground beef and onion. Place in Microwave safe container, cover and Microwave on HIGH for 9 minutes, stirring every 3 minutes until beef is done, add drained kidney beans and continue to heat, stirring regularly. Drain meat mixture and stir in chili powder. On tostadas, layer meat mixture, tomato, lettuce, avocado and cheese. Serve with taco sauce and sour cream. Yields 6 servings.

Fun Food Fact: *The Federal Trade Commission mandates the labeling of food containers. The ingredients must be listed on the label in order of the percentage of the total weight. The highest percentage is listed first.*

Cheeseburger Loaf

2 pounds ground beef
1 envelope onion soup mix
1/2 cup cracker crumbs
1/8 teaspoon pepper
1 egg, beaten
1/2 cup milk
1/2 pound Cheddar cheese, sliced
1/4 cup ketchup

Preparation Time!

Salad Page 32
Vegetable Page 52
Dessert Page 114
Set the table Page 125

Combine beef, soup mix, cracker crumbs, pepper, egg and milk. Spoon half of the mixture into a 9 x 5 loafpan.
Place cheese slices on top of meat mixture. Top with the remaining meat mixture, covering cheese. Put ketchup on
the top of the loaf. Bake at 350° for 1 hour and 15 minutes. Yields 8 servings.

Fun Food Fact: *Jell-o was created in 1897. Today 2 million boxes of Jell-o are sold daily.*

Too Easy Chicken and Dressing

4 chicken breasts, skinned
Salt
Pepper
1 (10 3/4-ounce) can cream of chicken soup, undiluted
1 (10 3/4-ounce) can cream of mushroom soup, undiluted
1 (8-ounce) package herb-seasoned stuffing mix
1/2 cup butter or margarine, melted

Preparation Time!

Salad Page 31
Vegetable Page 53
Dessert Page 117
Set the table Page 125

Place chicken breasts in shallow Microwave-safe dish. Add 1/2 cup water, cover and Microwave on HIGH for 20 minutes turning every 4 minutes. Cook thoroughly until done. Take the meat off of the bones and cut into medium pieces. Combine the two kinds of soup and add 2 cups of water, mix well. Mix the stuffing mix and the butter, setting 1/4 cup of the mixture aside for topping. In a 9 x 13 greased baking dish, layer half of the chicken, soup mixture, and stuffing. Repeat layers. Top with 1/4 cup stuffing mix. Cover and refrigerate until ready to bake. Bake uncovered at 350° for 40 minutes. Yields 8 servings.

Fun Food Fact: *The mushroom is a fungus. 400 growers in America produce 750 million pounds of mushrooms annually.*

Sloppy, Sloppy Joes

1 1/2 pounds ground beef
1 medium onion, chopped
1/4 cup green pepper, chopped
1 cup celery, chopped
1 (10 3/4-ounce) can tomato soup, undiluted
1 cup ketchup
1 teaspoon salt
1/8 teaspoon pepper
1 (8-buns) package hamburger buns
1 1/2 cups Cheddar cheese, grated

20 Min.

Preparation Time!

Vegetable Page 33
Dessert Page 118
Set the table Page 125

Place ground beef, onion, green pepper and celery in a Microwave safe dish. Cover and Microwave, stirring every 3 minutes until done. Drain. Stir in soup and ketchup, salt and pepper. Heat thoroughly in Microwave. Spoon over bun halves and top with cheese. Yields 16 servings.

Fun Food Fact: *Foods prepared according to Kosher laws do not allow meat and milk to be eaten together. There must be separate cooking untensils and dishes for preparing both.*

91

Chicken Spaghetti

6-8 chicken breasts
1 bay leaf
1 (8-ounce) package spaghetti, uncooked
1 medium onion, chopped
1/4 cup green pepper, chopped
1/3 cup celery, chopped
1/4 teaspoon garlic salt
3 tablespoons butter or margarine
1 (10 3/4-ounce) can cream of mushroom soup, undiluted
1 (28-ounce) can tomatoes, drained and chopped
1 teaspoon Worcestershire sauce
1/4 teaspoon tabasco sauce
1/8 teaspoon pepper
1/2 teaspoon salt
1 cup grated Cheddar cheese

45 Min.

Preparation Time!

Suggestions:
Salad — page 27
Desert — Page 123
Set the table — Page 125

Place chicken breasts and bay leaf in a Microwave safe dish. Cover and microwave on HIGH turning chicken breasts every four minutes until done. Let cool and discard bay leaf. Bone chicken and cut into medium pieces. Set aside in a large mixing bowl. Break spaghetti into 3 sections and place in Microwave safe dish. Cover spaghetti with water and cook on High until spaghetti is tender. Drain and add to chicken. In a Microwave safe dish add onion, green pepper, celery and butter. Cover and cook on HIGH until vegetables are tender. Add vegetable mixture to chicken and spaghetti. Toss and add garlic salt, mushroom soup, tomatoes, Worcestershire sauce, tabasco sauce, pepper and salt. Mix well and spoon into a greased 9 x 13 baking dish. Top with cheese. Bake at 350° for 20 minutes. Yields 8 servings.

Fun Food Fact: *Fish sticks were introduced by Edward Piszek of Philadelphia in 1946. He named them Mrs. Paul's Fish Sticks after one of his partners.*

Beef Stroganoff

1 (8-ounce) package egg noodles
1 1/2 pounds ground beef
3 green onions chopped
1 cup sliced fresh mushrooms
1 (10 3/4-ounce) can cream of mushroom soup
1/2 teaspoon parsley flakes
1 (8-ounce) carton sour cream
1 teaspoon salt
1/4 teaspoon pepper
1/2 cup grated cheddar cheese
Paprika

25 Min.

Preparation Time!

Bread Page 19
Salad Page 24
Dessert Page 121
Set the table Page 125

Place noodles in Microwave safe dish, adding water to cover noodles. Cover and Microwave on HIGH until noodles are tender, stirring gently every 3 minutes. Drain and set aside. Place ground beef, onion and mushrooms in Microwave safe dish, cover and Microwave on HIGH. Stir mixture every 3 minutes until done. Drain. Mix noodles, ground beef mixture, soup, parsley, sour cream, salt and pepper and pour mixture into greased 9 x 13 baking dish. Top with cheese and Paprika. Cover and bake at 350° for 35 minutes. Yields 6 servings.

Fun Food Fact: *Fettuccine Alfredo was created in 1914 by Alfredo DiLelio in his restaurant in Rome, Italy. The recipe was brought back to America by visiting honeymooners.*

Chicken Tacos

1 (8-ounce) package cream cheese, softened
1/3 cup milk
1 1/2 cup chopped chicken
1 (4-ounce) can chopped green chilies, drained
1/2 teaspoon salt
1/4 teaspoon chili powder
4 green onions chopped
10 taco shells
1 large tomato chopped
1 cup shredded lettuce
Black olives

20 Min.

Preparation Time!

Vegetables Page 57
Dessert Page 115
Set the table page 125

Combine cream cheese and milk in a Microwave safe dish. Heat on HIGH, stirring every 2 minutes until heated. Add chicken, chilies, salt, chili powder and onions. Fill tacos with meat mixture and add lettuce and tomato. Garnish with black olives and serve. Yields 10 servings.

Fun Food Fact: In America black olives are green olives that have been given a bath in lye and sugar with iron. This process turns them from green to black.

94

It looks like Spaghetti!

1 large spaghetti squash
1 medium onion, sliced into rings and separated
1/2 cup sliced green pepper
2 tablespoons butter or margarine
1 (3 1/2-ounce) package sliced pepperoni
1 (15-ounce) can tomato sauce
1 teaspoon dried whole oregano
1/8 teaspoon pepper
1/2 teaspoon garlic salt
1 teaspoon dried whole basil
1/2 cup grated Parmesan cheese

Preparation Time!

Salad Page 37
Dessert Page 124
Set the table page 125

Wash squash; cut in half. Place halves cut side down in a Microwave safe dish. Add 1/4 cup water. Cover and Microwave on HIGH for 8-10 minutes or until the strands can be removed with a fork. Drain squash and cool. Using a fork, remove spaghetti-like strands. Measure 5 cups of strands and set aside. Place onion, green pepper and butter in a Microwave safe dish, cover and Microwave on HIGH stirring every two minutes until tender. Add pepperoni and cook 2 more minutes. Stir in tomato sauce, oregano, garlic salt, pepper and basil. Cover and Microwave 4 minutes on HIGH. Toss with squash strands and sprinkle with Parmesan cheese. Yields 8 servings.

Fun Food Fact: *European settlers were introduced to squashes by the Indians. There are many different varieties of squash like yellow crookneck, scalloped, zucchini, butternut and acorn squash. In the produce department of many grocery stores you can see as many as six different kinds of squash.*

Flaky Chicken

1 cup corn flakes, mashed
1/2 teaspoon salt
1/2 teaspoon celery salt
1/4 teaspoon garlic salt
1/2 teaspoon paprika
1/2 teaspoon parsley
4 chicken breasts, skinned
1/2 cup milk

20 Min.

Preparation Time!

Salad Page 34
Vegetables Page 58
Dessert Page 114
Set the table Page 125

Combine first 6 ingredients, mixing well. Dip chicken in milk and roll in corn flake mixture, coating well. Place chicken in greased 9 x 13 baking dish. Bake uncovered in oven at 350° for 45 minutes or until chicken is tender. Yields 4 servings.

Fun Food Fact: *In 1907 Will Keith Kellogg created one of the most popular cereals in history. Kellogg's Toasted Corn Flakes remains popular today and is eaten by great-grandchildren of the first corn flake cereal eaters.*

Pork Chops

4 pork chops
1/3 cup Dijon mustard
1 lemon, cut in half
1/4 teaspoon garlic powder
1/2 teaspoon salt
1/8 teaspoon pepper
1 cup chopped fresh parsley
4 teaspoons cracker crumbs

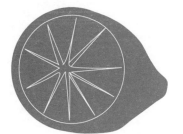

Preparation Time!

Salad Page 28
Vegetable Page 50
Dessert Page 122
Set the table Page 125

Wash pork chops and spread each side with mustard. Combine garlic powder, salt, pepper, parsley, and crumbs. Coat both sides of each pork chop. Place in greased 9 x 9 baking dish and squeeze the juice of half of a lemon over pork chops. Cover with foil and bake at 350° for 30 minutes or until pork chops are done. Garnish with lemon slices. Yields 4 servings.

Fun Food Fact: America produces over 80% of the world's crop of grapefruit. Florida produces the most with more than 3 1/2 billion pounds coming from that state alone. Grapefruit was introduced first in Florida in 1823.

Taco Taters

4 baking potatoes
1 pound ground beef
1/2 cup chopped onion
1 (1 1/4-ounce) package taco seasoning mix
1 cup water
1/2 cup sour cream

25 Min.

Preparation Time!

Salad Page 24
Dessert Page 117
Set the table Page 125

Wash potatoes, bake in oven at 400° for 1 hour or until soft when pierced with a fork. Place ground beef and onion in Microwave safe dish, cover and Microwave on High, stirring every two minutes, until done. Drain well. Add seasoning mix and water. Cover and Microwave on HIGH for 4 minutes, stirring every two minutes. Split tops of potatoes and fluff potato with a fork. Spoon beef mixture over potatoes and top with sour cream. Yields 4 servings.

Fun Food Fact: *Long before there were ovens, people cooked their food with rocks heated in a fire and placed in a basket around or on top of the food. In South America there are tribes that still cook many of their dishes with hot rocks.*

Hobo Dinners

6 (10" squares) aluminum foil (1 for each serving)
1 1/2 pounds ground beef
Salt
Pepper
2 medium onions, sliced into thick slices
3 large red potatoes, cut in half

Preparation Time!

Salad Page 25
Dessert Page 115
Set the table Page 125

To each square of aluminum foil add one patty of ground beef, sprinkle patty with salt and pepper. Add one thick slice of onion and top with one half of a scrubbed red potato. Pull the sides of the foil up around the top of the potato and fold the edges down making a secure seal. Do the same with the ends and seal again. Be sure that the seals are on top of the bundle so that the fluids and steam will be trapped inside for basting. Bake at 350° for 45 minutes or until done. Be careful unwrapping the dinners avoiding the steam. These can be cooked out on the grill for a picnic too! Yields 6 servings.

Fun Food Fact: Wild rice is not a true rice. It is a grain grown from a tall aquatic grass growing in the northern part of America.

Gumbo Pork Chops

4-6 pork chops
Salt
Pepper
1 (10 3/4-ounce) can chicken gumbo soup
1 1/2 cups of water
1 cup rice, uncooked
Parsley

Preparation Time!

Salad Page 32
Vegetable Page 54
Dessert Page 122
Set the table Page 125

Wash pork chops and salt and pepper both sides. Mix soup, water and rice. Pour into greased 9 x 13 baking dish and place pork chops on top of rice mixture. Sprinkle with parsley. Cover and bake at 350° for 50 minutes or until liquid has been absorbed and pork chops are done. Yields 4-6 servings.

*Chicken breasts could be used instead of pork chops

Fun Food Fact: *Americans buy over 12 billion gallons of colas every year.*

Potato Chip Casserole

Preparation Time!

Salad Page 36
Dessert Page 123
Set the table Page 125

4 cups cooked chopped chicken
4 tablespoons lemon juice
3/4 cup mayonnaise
1 teaspoon salt
1/2 teaspoon seasoning salt
2 cups chopped celery
4 hard-boiled eggs, sliced
1 (10 3/4-ounce) can cream of chicken soup
1 chopped onion
1 cup grated Cheddar cheese
1 1/2 cups crushed potato chips

Mix chicken, lemon juice, mayonnaise, salt and seasoning salt. Add celery, eggs, soup, onion and mix well. Pour into greased 9 x 13 baking dish. Top with grated cheese and potato chips. Bake at 350° for 30 minutes. Yields 8 servings.

Fun Food Fact: *The pineapple was first discovered by Columbus on the island of Guadeloupe in 1493. He called it the "Pine of the Indians."*

Hearty Meat and Potatoes

1 1/2 pounds ground beef
4 medium red potatoes
1/4 cup chopped onion
1 teaspoon parsley
1 teaspoon salt
1/4 teaspoon pepper
3 cups grated Cheddar cheese
1 1/2 cups milk
Paprika

Preparation Time!

Salad Page 38
Dessert Page 124
Set the table Page 125

Make hamburger patties out of ground beef; about 1/2" thick. Place hamburger patties in bottom of greased 9 x 13 baking dish. Peel and slice potatoes. Add onion, parsley, salt and pepper, toss potatoes to coat with seasoning and layer potatoes on hamburger patties. Add grated cheese and pour milk over the top. Sprinkle with paprika. Cover dish with foil and bake at 400° for 60 minutes or until potatoes are tender and hamburger is done. Yields 6 servings.

Fun Food Fact: On the average, Americans drink more soft drinks than water or any other beverage.

102

Stuffed Cornish Game Hens

Preparation Time!

4 Cornish Game Hens
Salt
Pepper
1 (8-ounce) package herb-seasoned stuffing mix
1 (10 3/4-ounce) can cream of mushroom soup
1/2 teaspoon garlic salt
4 tablespoons butter or margarine, melted
4 tablespoons parsley
1/2 cup water

Salad Page 27
Dessert Page 123
Set the table Page 125

Wash hens and remove parts from inside of bird. Sprinkle outside generously with salt and pepper. In a bowl mix stuffing, soup, garlic salt, butter and parsley. Stuff each hen with mixture. Place hens in greased 9 x 13 baking dish. Add 1/2 cup water and cover with foil. Bake at 350° for 50 minutes or until tender and legs pull away from sides easily. Yields 4 servings.

Fun Food Fact: *The first McDonald's opened in San Bernardino, California just prior to World War II.*

Hot Dog Sandwiches

8 Hot dogs
8 slices of white or wheat bread
Butter or margarine softened
Prepared mustard
8 slices American cheese
1/4 cup butter or margarine, melted

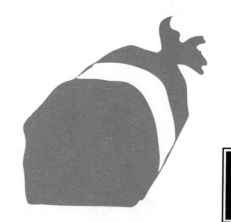

15 Min.

Preparation Time!

Soup Page 43
Dessert Page 116
Set the table Page 125

Place hot dogs in Microwave safe dish. Cover and Microwave on HIGH for 4 minutes, turning once. Spread butter and then mustard on one side of each slice of bread. Layer cheese on top of mustard. Place one hot dog with ends pointing to the corners. Pull up each side and secure with a toothpick. Drizzle with melted butter and bake at 350° for 5 minutes. Yields 8 servings.

Fun Food Fact: *Americans consumption of rice has more than doubled in the past 20 years. We consume over 20 pounds of rice per person yearly.*

Chicken Cordon Blue

4 chicken breasts, boned and skinned
4 slices of ham
4 slices of Swiss cheese
1 teaspoon parsley
1/8 teaspoon pepper
1 egg beaten
Italian bread crumbs
1/4 cup margarine
1 (10 1/4-ounce) cream of mushroom soup
1 cup sour cream
1/3 cup dry cooking sherry

25 Min.

Preparation Time!

Salad Page 35
Vegetable Page 67
Dessert Page 123
Set the table Page 125

Pound chicken to 1/4" thickness. Place one slice of ham and one slice of cheese on top of each chicken breast. Roll up breasts and secure with a toothpick. Dip each rolled up chicken breast in egg and roll in bread crumbs, place in greased 9 x 13 baking dish. Drizzle breasts with melted butter. Mix parsley, pepper, soup, sour cream and cooking sherry. Spoon mixture around chicken beasts. Bake at 350° for 45 minutes or until chicken is done. Yields 4 servings.

Fun Food Fact: Quinine gives Tonic Water it's distinctive flavor. Quinine comes from the bark of a tree that grows in the South American rain forests. It was useful in the treatment of malaria. Athletes believe drinking tonic water will keep muscles from cramping during physical exertion.

Island Chicken

6 chicken breasts, skin and bones removed
Pepper
6 slices bacon
1 (2 1/2-ounce) package dried beef
1 (10 3/4-ounce) can of cream of chicken soup
1 1/2 cups sour cream
1 (8-ounce) package cream cheese

25 Min.

Preparation Time!

Salad Page 26
Vegetable Page 64
Dessert Page 124
Set the table Page 125

Lightly sprinkle chicken breasts with pepper on both sides. Wrap each breast with one piece of bacon. Layer dried beef in bottom of 9 x 13 baking dish. Place wrapped chicken breasts on top of dried beef. Mix soup and sour cream. Open cream cheese and cut into 1/2" cubes. Mix with soup mixture and pour over chicken breasts. Cover dish with foil and bake at 350° for 1 1/2 hours.   Yields 6 servings.

Fun Food Fact: *Graham crackers were named after Reverend Sylvester Graham in the 1830's. He believed that healthy nutrition was a must and set up many restaurants that served only the healthiest of meals.*

Spiced Crispy Chicken

1 cut-up chicken fryer
1/3 cup soy sauce
3 tablespoons salad oil
1/4 teaspoon garlic powder
1 teaspoon ginger
1/4 teaspoon pepper

10 Min.

Preparation Time!

Salad Page 34
Vegetable Page 73
Dessert Page 114
Set the table Page 125

Wash chicken parts and pat dry with paper towels. Place chicken in greased 9 x 13 baking dish. Mix remaining ingredients in bowl and brush on chicken. Cover and let chicken sit in refrigerator for 30 minutes or longer. Remove dish from refrigerator and place in cold oven. Turn oven on and bake at 350° for 50 minutes. Brush chicken again with soy sauce mixture halfway during baking. Be sure to use oven mitts when removing baking dish. Remember that the sides of the dish are hot. Finish baking uncovered. Yields 4 servings.

Fun Food Fact: In America ice cream has been around since 1744. However, the Greeks and Romans used mountain snow and ice to cool their wine.

Pizza Spaghetti

1 (4-ounce) package sliced pepperoni
1 chopped onion
3 tablespoons butter or margarine
1 (6-ounce) package vermicelli
2 (8-ounce) cans tomato sauce
1/2 teaspoon oregano
1/2 teaspoon basil
1 teaspoon Worcestershire sauce
1/3 cup Parmesan cheese
8 ounces sliced Mozzarella cheese

35 Min.

Preparation Time!

Salad Page 24
Dessert Page 117
Set the table Page 125

Place pepperoni slices in Microwave safe dish, add 1/2 cup water. Cover and Microwave on HIGH for 3 minutes. Drain off water and set aside. Place onion and butter in Microwave safe dish. Cover and Microwave on HIGH for 3 minutes. To the onion and butter add tomato sauce, oregano, basil. Mix well and set aside. Break the spaghetti into 3 sections and place in Microwave safe dish. Add 3 cups water and Microwave on HIGH for 15 minutes, stirring every 3 minutes until spaghetti is tender. Drain off excess water and rinse spaghetti in colander, removing excess fluids. Toss the spaghetti with Worcestershire sauce and Parmesan cheese. Put the spaghetti in the bottom of a greased 9 x 13 baking dish. Arrange the pepperoni slices on top of the spaghetti. Pour the tomato sauce mixture over the pepperoni and add the sliced Mozzarella cheese. Bake at 350° for 25 minutes.

Fun Food Fact: *Yogurt is a creamy food made with milk that has been curdled with a bacteria. It has been around since the 1500's and is believed to have come from Turkey.*

Your Own BBQ Chicken

1 chicken fryer, cut into parts.
2 cups ketchup
1/4 cup brown sugar
1/4 cup Worcestershire sauce
1/4 cup yellow mustard
1/4 cup finely chopped onion
1/4 teaspoon garlic powder
2 tablespoons lemon juice
1/4 teaspoon salt
1/8 teaspoon pepper

20 Min.

Preparation Time!

Salad Page 36
Vegetable Page 66
Dessert Page 119
Set the table Page 125

Wash chicken parts, pat dry and place in 9 x 13 baking dish. Mix remaining ingredients and pour over chicken. Cover dish with foil and bake at 350° for 55 minutes or until done. Yields 4 servings.

Fun Food Fact: *The Jewfish is a grouper found in the waters around Florida and in the Gulf Sea. They can weight up to 700 pounds each. Imagine the number of people you could feed if you caught just one 300-400 pound fish!*

Ham with Lemon Sauce

1 lemon
1/2 cup brown sugar
1 tablespoon yellow mustard
1 (10-12-ounce) slice of ham, 1/2" thick

Preparation Time!

Salad Page 30
Vegetable Page 61
Dessert Page 124
Set the table Page 125

Grate peel of one lemon. Cut lemon in half and squeeze the juice from one half. Slice the other half into thin slices. Combine peel, juice, brown sugar and mustard. Mix well. Layer sauce on top of cooked ham. Top with lemon slices and bake at 425° for 15 minutes. Yields 4 servings.

Fun Food Fact: *What makes brown sugar brown? It is less refined than white sugar and contains crystals of molasses syrup.*

Swiss Chicken Breasts

8 chicken breasts, skin and bones removed
8 slices Swiss cheese
1 (10 3/4-ounce) can cream of mushroom soup
1/4 dry white cooking wine
1 cup herb-seasoned stuffing mix, crushed
1/4 cup butter or margarine, melted

Preparation Time!

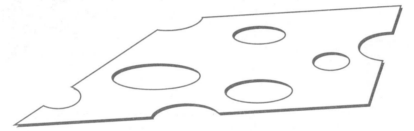

Salad Page 26
Vegetable Page 55
Dessert Page 115
Set the table Page 125

Arrange chicken in greased 9 x 13 baking dish. Top with cheese slices. Mix soup and wine and spoon over chicken. Sprinkle with stuffing mix. Drizzle melted butter over crumbs. Bake at 350° for 50 minutes. Yields 8 servings

Fun Food Fact: *Parsley is a herb used in many recipes included in this cookbook. Fresh parsley can be grown from a package of seeds. Plant the parsley in a pot and keep near a sunny window. Snip leaves with kitchen shears and wash before adding to recipes.*

Breakfast Enchiladas

1/2 pound ground sausage
2 potatoes, peeled and grated
3/4 cup chopped green pepper
1/2 cup chopped onion
8 eggs beaten
2 1/2 cups Cheddar cheese, grated
8 (8-inch) flour tortillas
1/4 cup butter or margarine, melted
Picante sauce

35 Min.

Preparation Time!

Salad Page 24
Set the table Page 125

Place sausage in a Microwave safe dish, cover and Microwave on HIGH, stirring every 2 minutes until done, drain and set aside. Place potatoes, pepper, and onion in Microwave safe dish and Microwave, stirring every 2 minutes until done. Add eggs and continue to Microwave, still stirring every 2 minutes. Add sausage and 2 cups of grated cheese to egg mixture. Spoon equal amounts of mixture into tortillas; roll up. Place tortillas in greased 9 x 13 baking dish seam side down. Brush with melted butter and top with remaining cheese. Cover dish with foil and bake at 350° for 15 minutes. Serve with picante sauce.

Fun Food Fact: Brunch means breakfast with lunch. It is a meal eaten in late morning. Brunch is believed to have been started by the English after hunting in the morning.

112

Make Ahead Breakfast

6 slices of bread
Butter or margarine
1 pound ground pork sausage
2 cups grated Cheddar cheese
6 eggs beaten
2 cups half and half
1 teaspoon salt
1/8 teaspoon pepper
1/4 teaspoon parsley
Paprika

20 Min.

Preparation Time!

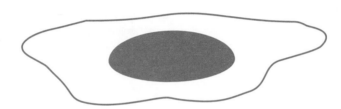

Salad Page 29
Set the table Page 125

Remove crusts from bread; spread bread with butter and place butter side up in a greased 9 x 13 baking dish. Place sausage in Microwave safe dish and cover. Microwave on HIGH for 9 minutes, stirring every three minutes until done. Drain well and spoon sausage over bread and top with grated cheese. Mix eggs, half and half, salt, pepper and parsley. Pour mixture over cheese, and sprinkle top with paprika. Cover and refrigerate until ready to cook. Bake uncovered at 350° for 45 minutes. Yields 8 servings.

Fun Food Fact: *Americans eat an average of 19 pounds of pasta each year. 170 million pounds of durum wheat, used for grinding into semolina flour is exported to Italy for making pasta each year.*

Fruity Pizza

1 (20-ounce) package refrigerated Sugar cookie dough
1 (8-ounce) package cream cheese, softened
1/3 cup sugar
1/2 teaspoon vanilla
Sliced fresh bananas, kiwi, strawberries, grapes
1 (11-ounce) can of mandarin oranges, drained
Apricot preserves

Preparation Time!

Grease a 14" pizza pan. Spread the cookie dough evenly, covering the top of the pan. Bake at 350° for 15 minutes. Cool. Mix cream cheese, sugar and vanilla. Spread mixture over cooled crust. Arrange fruit around the outside working towards the center. Create your own design. With a food brush, paint the fruit with Apricot preserves. Chill and cut into wedges. Yields 12 servings

Fun Food Fact: *The kiwi fruit originated in China and was brought to America in 1904. It is named after the Kiwi bird of New Zealand.*

114

Snowballs

1 1/2 cups canned sweetened coconut
4 scoops lemon sherbert
1/2 cup chocolate syrup

Place coconut on cookie sheet and toast in oven for 10 minutes or until brown. Place coconut on wax paper to cool.
Roll scoops of ice cream in coconut and place in serving dish. Keep covered and in the freezer until ready to serve.
Heat chocolate syrup in microwave and pour over snowballs. Yields 4 servings.

Fun Food Fact: *Lobsters in colonial days grew to record sizes. The largest one on record weighed 42 pounds and was caught in 1935. Now the average American lobster weighs between 1 and 1 1/2 pounds.*

Quick and Easy Banana Pudding

1 (6-ounce) package instant vanilla pudding mix
1 (12-ounce) container frozen whipped topping
Vanilla wafers
4 bananas, sliced

Preparation Time!

Prepare instant vanilla pudding according to directions on box. Mix bananas and whipped topping into pudding and layer pudding with Vanilla wafers. Repeat layers until all of pudding mixture is used. Top with Vanilla wafers and refrigerate until serving.

Fun Food Fact: *Beta carotene is found in vegetables like kale and broccoli. The body converts Beta carotene to Vitamin A.*

Dirty Ice Cream

4 scoops vanilla ice cream
1 1/2 cup chopped pecans
Chocolate syrup

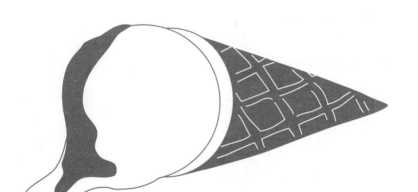

Roll each scoop of ice cream in chopped pecan and place in serving dish. Keep frozen until ready to serve. Top with chocolate syrup. Yields 4 servings.

Fun Food Fact: *Lemons are native to Asia. Today most of the lemons grown in America come from California.*

Easy Trifle

1 (6-ounce) package instant vanilla pudding
2 packages ladyfingers
1 (10/12-ounce) package frozen raspberries, thawed
3 bananas, sliced
3 kiwi, peeled and sliced
2 (11-ounce) cans mandarin oranges, drained

Preparation Time!

Mix pudding with 3 cups cold milk and set aside. In a glass trifle bowl, layer ladyfingers on the bottom and along sides. Drizzle ladyfingers with frozen raspberries. Layer pudding on top of raspberries and ladyfingers. Add bananas, kiwi and mandarin oranges. Place another layer of ladyfingers on top of the fruit and drizzle with raspberries. Layer pudding on top and add remaining fruit. Chill and serve. Yields 8 servings.

Fun Food Fact: John Chapman was born in 1774 in Massachusetts. Known as Johnny Appleseed, he planted apple trees from Massachusetts to Fort Wayne, Indiana.

118

Blondies

1/4 cup shortening
1/3 cup butter or margarine, softened
1/2 cup sugar
1/2 cup firmly packed brown sugar
1 egg
1 teaspoon vanilla extract
1 1/2 cups all-purpose flour
1/2 teaspoon salt
1 (6 ounce) package semi-sweet chocolate morsels
1 (6 ounce) package butterscotch morsels
1/2 cup chopped pecans

Preparation Time!

Cream shortening, butter, sugar and brown sugar. Beat in egg and vanilla. Add remaining ingredients and mix well. Spread into greased 9 x 13 pan. Bake at 350° for 20 -25 minutes and cool. Cut into squares. Yields 4 dozen

Fun Food Fact: *Vanilla beans are from orchids. They are long brown pods from 6-12" in length.*

Abe's Peanut Butter Logs

1 3/4 cups sifted powdered sugar
1/4 cup butter or margarine, softened
1 cup crunchy peanut butter
2 cups crisp rice cereal
1 can chocolate frosting

20 Min.

Preparation Time!

Combine powdered sugar and butter in mixing bowl, mixing until smooth. Stir in peanut butter and cereal, mixing thoroughly. Shape mixture into little log shapes, about 1/2" wide by 1 1/2" long and place on wax paper. Chill and spread tops with chocolate frosting. Yields 7 dozen.

Fun Food Fact: On an average each American eats almost 11 pounds of chocolate per year. Not much when you consider we eat 26 lbs or more of cheese a year.

Razzberry Bars

1 cup margarine, softened
1 cup sugar
2 egg yolks
1/2 teaspoon vanilla extract
2 cups all-purpose flour
1 cup chopped walnuts
1/2 cup raspberry preserves

Preparation Time!

Cream margarine; gradually adding sugar, beating until light and fluffy. Add egg yolks and vanilla. Blend well. Add flour and mix thoroughly. Stir in nuts. Spread about 1/3 of the mixture in a greased 9" square baking pan. Drop raspberry preserves by the spoonfuls over batter and spread till near the edges of pan. Cover the preserves with the remaining flour mixture. Crumble the mixture and let it drop on the top. Bake at 350° for 25 minutes or until golden brown. Cool and cut into squares. Yields 24 squares.

Fun Food Fact: Surimi is a fish paste developed in Japan. It is a method for shaping inexpensive fish to resemble more expensive varieties. In America we see it in the grocery store as imitation crab legs.

Make Ahead Chocolate Eclair Cake

2 (3-ounce) packages instant French Vanilla pudding
3 cups milk
1 (8-ounce) container frozen whipped topping
1 (16-ounce) box graham crackers
1 can chocolate frosting

Preparation Time!

Mix pudding and milk, blend until thick. Add whipped topping and mix again. In a 9 x 13 baking dish, layer graham crackers, breaking where necessary to make them fit. Place 1/2 of the pudding mixture on top of graham crackers. Layer graham crackers again and top with remaining pudding. Place more graham crackers on top of a piece of wax paper and spread crackers with chocolate frosting. Pick these frosted graham crackers up by the sides and place on top of final layer of pudding. Cover and refrigerate overnight. Yields 12 servings.

Fun Food Fact: *Nasturtiums are an edible flower. You can grow them in the garden and add them to salads or use as a garnish. They add a dash of color and have a peppery taste.*

Pretty Orange Cups

2 navel oranges
Orange sherbert
4 tablespoon orange juice
Mint leaves

Preparation Time!

Cut oranges in half and remove orange pulp, leaving the outside rind. Fill the orange halves with orange sherbert. Wrap in plastic and place in freezer until ready to serve. Remove plastic, place in serving dish and pour 1 tablespoon orange juice on the top of each orange half. Garnish with fresh mint leaf. Yields 4 servings. You are not limited to orange sherbert in this recipe. You could use chocolate, vanilla ice cream or even raspberry sherbert.

Fun Food Fact: *Mint grows in almost every state in America. It makes an easy garnish for drinks and desserts. Plant a sprig in the sun near your home for easy access. It is fun to rub a leaf in your fingers and smell the fresh scent.*

Recipe For Family First Aid Kit

*The Mid-South **SAFE KIDS** Coalition recommends the following items to be included in making your own First Aid Kit. This kit can be assembled as a family activity that includes teaching children what the items are for and how to use the items in the event of an injury.*

- Bandaids in assorted sizes to dress small cuts
- Sterile gauze pads to dress large cuts
- Adhesive tape to hold gauze pads in place
- Scissors to cut adhesive tape
- A triangular bandage and several safety pins to make a sling
- An elastic bandage to wrap sprains
- Tweezers to remove splinters, bee stings
- Rubbing alcohol to sterilize "tweezers"
- Baking soda or calamine lotion to treat insect bites or poison ivy
- Hydrogen peroxide to clean cuts
- Cotton balls to use with hydrogen peroxide when cleaning cuts
- Thermometer to check for fever
- Acetomenophen (tylenol) to reduce fever
- Ipecac to induce vomiting in case of poisoning (call local Poison Control Center first)
- Icebag or Icepack kept in freezer to reduce swelling

How To Do It!

♦ To coat with crumbs - Place crumbs on wax paper and roll meat or chicken on crumbs to make them stick.

♦ Drain - Pour the cooking liquids off of the meat or vegetables by tilting the cooking dish with the top ajar just enough to let the liquids out and keep the vegetables in. Use a colander if the pieces of food are bigger than the holes in the colander or stainer.

♦ Melt Butter - Remove paper from butter and place in Microwave safe dish. Heat on HIGH to melt (about one or two minutes.)

♦ Cook Chicken - Place chicken with thick sides positioned to the outside on the Microwave safe dish. Cover and Microwave on HIGH for 4 minutes. Move chicken around and turn dish. Cover and Microwave again. Repeat until chicken is tender and cooked.

♦ Drizzle - Spoon liquid over chicken or vegetables.

♦ Grease Pan - Take a tablespoon of butter or margarine and hold with paper towel. Move around bottom and sides of baking dish.

♦ Cook Bacon - Take slices of bacon out of package and lay on bacon-cooking dish. Cover with paper towels and Microwave on HIGH for 4 minutes turn and repeat until bacon is crisp. Remove paper towels and let bacon cool before removing from dish.

♦ Soften butter or cream cheese - Remove paper or foil and place in Microwave safe dish. Microwave on low setting for a short time. Turn and repeat until softened.

♦ Pound Meat - Lay pieces of meat on wax paper and use the edge of a saucer to tenderize by gently tapping meat. This breaks the fibers in the beef or chicken.

For Additional Copies of "Hey Mom...I'll Cook Dinner"

For additional copies of this publication or other Impressions Ink publications, please return to the location where this book was purchased. If it was purchased while traveling or was given as a gift, we will be happy to suggest a store in your area that carries our publications. Call 1-800-388-5382, 8:00 a.m. to 5:00 p.m., CST, Monday-Friday.

To Order Direct:

"Hey Mom...I'll Cook Dinner" $15.95

"Dinner Will Be Ready In A Minute" $15.95

(shipping & handling included)

Specify Qty:
_____
_____

You can order direct by sending a check to: Impressions Ink • 5147 Patrick Henry Drive • Memphis, TN 38134

Ship To:

Name: _____

Mailing Address: _____

City: _____ State: _____ Zip: _____

Telephone Number: _____

How did you receive your copy of "Hey Mom...I'll Cook Dinner"?

Purchased in Retail Store ☐   Store Name: _____ City: _____ State: _____

Received as a Gift ☐   Other (please specify): _____

All of us at Impressions Ink appreciate your interest in our products.

Our Pledge – We will do our best to provide quality products and a level of service that will surprise and please you.